WRITERS AND THEIR WORK

ISOBEL ARMSTRONG
*General Editor*

# OLIVE SENIOR

# OLIVE SENIOR

## Denise deCaires Narain

NORTHCOTE
●● BRITISH
●● COUNCIL

© Copyright 2011 Denise deCaires Narain

First published in 2011 by Northcote House Publishers Ltd, Horndon, Tavistock, Devon, PL19 9NQ, United Kingdom.
Tel: +44 (0) 1822 810066  Fax: +44 (0) 1822 810034.

**British Library Cataloguing-in-Publication Data**
A catalogue record for this book is available from the British Library

ISBN 978-0-7463-1094-6 hardcover
ISBN 978-0-7463-1099-1 paperback

Typeset by PDQ Typesetting, Newcastle-under-Lyme
Printed and bound in the United Kingdom

In memory of Dennis Justin deCaires
& Percy Carl Narain

# Contents

# Biographical Outline

| | |
|---|---|
| 1941 | Born Olive Marjorie Senior, 23 December, Troy, Jamaica; daughter of Reginald Senior (a small farmer) and Edna Peart. Educated at Montego Bay Secondary High School. |
| 1967 | Bachelor of Journalism, Carleton University, Ottawa, Canada. |
| 1967–89 | Worked in the field of communications and book publishing as freelancer and researcher. Editor of *Social and Economic Studies* (1972–7) and editor of *Jamaica Journal* (1982–9). |
| 1979 | Centenary Medal for contribution to Literature, Institute of Jamaica, followed by Silver Medal (1987) and Gold (2004). |
| 1985 | *Talking of Trees* published. |
| 1986 | *Summer Lightning and Other Stories* published. |
| 1987 | Commonwealth Writers Prize for *Summer Lightning*. |
| 1989 | *Arrival of the Snake-Woman and Other Stories* published. |
| 1989–92 | Worked as freelance writer and creative writing teacher in Europe. Writing fellow and writer in residence in the Caribbean, North America and Europe. |
| 1991 | *Working Miracles: Women's Lives in the English-Speaking Caribbean* published. |
| 1992–present | Migrated to Canada, works as freelance writer and lecturer. Conducts writing workshops in the Caribbean and Europe. |
| 1994 | *Gardening in the Tropics* published. Hawthornden Fellow, USA. |

| | |
|---|---|
| 1995 | *Discerner of Hearts and Other Stories* published. |
| | F. G. Bressani Literary Prize for Poetry. |
| 1994–5 | Dana Distinguished Professor of Creative Writing and International Education, St Lawrence University, Canton New York. |
| 2003 | Norman Manley Washington Foundation Award for Excellence (preservation of Jamaican culture). |
| 2004 | *Encyclopedia of Jamaican Heritage* published. |
| 2005 | Annual Phillip Sherlock Lecture, University of the West Indies, Mona Campus, Jamaica. |
| | *Over the Roofs of the World* published. |
| 2007 | *Shell* published. |

# Abbreviations and References

ASW   *Arrival of the Snake-Woman and Other Stories*
EJH   *Encyclopedia of Jamaican Heritage*
DH    *Discerner of Hearts and Other Stories*
GT    *Gardening in the Tropics*
ORW   *Over the Roofs of the World*
SL    *Summer Lightning and Other Stories*
TT    *Talking of Trees*
WM    *Working Miracles*

# 1

## Locating Olive Senior's Work

Olive Senior has published widely across a range of genres: her work to date includes four collections of poetry, three collections of short stories and at least four works of non-fiction as well as many shorter publications of various kinds in a range of anthologies, journals and newspapers. Her published work spans some 35 years: her first book was published in 1972 and her most recent was published in 2007 and a novel and illustrated children's book are forthcoming. This book explores this body of work as it intersects with a range of cultural and literary contexts and debates. In this chapter, I outline some of the most relevant literary and critical contexts and offer an overview of her preoccupations as a writer. Chapter 2 discusses a selection of stories from Senior's three collections focused on some of the key themes they address: childhood, the intersecting vectors of race, class and gender, and the representation of community. Chapter 3 focuses on a selection of short stories that are concerned with constructions of femininity and masculinity as they intersect with and are impacted by sexuality and ethnicity. Chapter 4 explores the main concerns of Senior's four collections of poetry focusing specifically on her persistent interest in the natural world and on land as an imperilled but crucial resource for the cultural and economic survival of Caribbean people. Chapter 5 discusses those poems and stories that foreground the labouring Caribbean subject, including migrant figures, and explores the connection Senior establishes between labour, craft and writing. Chapter 6 attends to Senior's considerable body of non-fiction writing, sociological and archival works that provide a fascinating supplement to her prose and poetry. The strength, diversity and range of her output across several decades makes hers a significant and distinctive contribution to Caribbean literature and culture and consolidates her position as one of the finest contemporary writers in the region.

Senior was born in 1941 in 'Cockpit Country' a rural, landlocked area of Jamaica. She grew up and was educated in Jamaica but spent a year in Canada studying journalism. In 1992 she relocated to Toronto, Canada, where she now resides, though she regularly spends periods of time in Jamaica. Asked in an interview about the impact of relocation on her writing, she says, 'But everything I write is about the Caribbean. I've never written another word about anywhere else.'[1] And indeed, there are remarkably few references to Canadian landscapes or culture in her work. This 'dislocated locatedness' is a defining feature of Caribbean history and literary culture and of Senior's oeuvre. It is still the case that many contemporary Caribbean writers have to leave the region to maintain careers as writers so that questions of location and belonging are recurring themes in the region, as are related issues of 'voice' and audience. Senior's writing offers nuanced and understated contributions to these debates, modulating the dominant notion of the Caribbean literary voice as a loudly protesting voice as well as questioning the celebratory tone surrounding many postcolonial discussions of migrant and Creole/hybrid identity. A brief outline of these cultural debates is useful here to contextualize Senior's significance as a writer.

The historical context of the anglophone Caribbean is one of violent conquest and destruction. Columbus' 'discovery' of the New World in 1492 was rapidly followed by the decimation of the Arawak, Carib, Taino and other indigenous peoples by a combination of violent repression, exposure to European diseases, and brutal labour regimes. As the Barbadian novelist, George Lamming, puts it, 'what we know about the modern Caribbean is that it is an area of the world that began with an almost unprecedented act of genocide.'[2] Decades of buccaneering and piracy and the cavalier exchanging of 'ownership' of the islands between European powers were eventually replaced by settlement and the establishment of plantations in the 1700s on the islands and on the mainland of South America. In 'Auction', Senior offers a succinct indictment of the greed motivating what she wryly terms a 'poetics of possessions':

> The poetics of men who rose from nothing but auctions
> from slave-ships, from piracy and smuggling, who pulled
> themselves up by the canestalk, rattooned rich as eastern
> potentates, retiring to England to don furs and golden
> chains of office...
>
> (*Shell*: 82)

Large-scale mono-crop production (sugar cane, tobacco, cotton, cocoa, rice) to maximize profits for the 'mother country' required considerable labour. From 1562 until 1833 when slavery was abolished, this labour was extracted from millions of enslaved African men, women and children (estimates range from 5 million upwards). Following abolition, people were brought from India (and, in fewer numbers from China and Madeira) to work in miserable conditions as indentured labourers. Africans brought as slaves were not allowed to practice their religious and cultural forms while Indian indentured labourers *were*, on the colonialist assumption that Indians were more 'civilized' but also as a strategy for managing this labour force better. This orchestrated 'racial divide' was consolidated by a wide range of structurally divisive policies that ensured an ethnically-charged demographic within the West Indian colonies, which continues to generate tensions. That many Caribbean nations adopted independence mottos that resonate with hopes for 'unity-in-diversity' attests to the enduring power of this divisive racial hierarchy. Jamaica gained independence in August 1962 and, despite its motto, 'Out of many, one people' it, like many other nations in the region, remains fractured by ethno-cultural divisions. This tense reality often remains disguised by the enduring myth of the Caribbean as a fashionably hybrid space in which all ethnicities have been happily creolized.

Gender relations also remain an area of contention. Historical accounts of slavery and its aftermath tended, until the mid-1980s, to take the male subject as normative and sociological and anthropological studies often focused on the *emasculating* impact of this history and, in seeking to rectify this, privileged the black male as the archetypal figure of resistance. Peter Wilson's influential *Crab Antics* (1973), for example, was structured around an argument that Caribbean men occupied outside/ public spaces, associated with *reputation*, while women occupied

inside/domestic spaces, associated with *respectability*. 'Reputation' and 'respectability' aligned with distinct value systems: the
indigenous and internally generated on the one hand ('nativist'/
male) and the colonially-inherited, externally driven on the
other ('foreign'/female). Wilson's model, as Jean Besson argues,
implies 'that cultural resistance to colonial culture is therefore
confined to Afro-Caribbean males'.[3] By the time Besson makes
this critique, other work had been published which effectively
put gender on the agenda, generating an extensive body of
research that allowed the impact of enslavement as a gendered
process to be analysed.[4] More recent work argues that plantation
slavery so violently ruptured African socio-familial structures as
to effectively 'de-gender' both enslaved men and women.
Treated as 'chattel' (literally, 'moveable property') of the
plantation owner, the suggestion here is that feminist inter-
pretations of gender require fundamental re-thinking in a
context in which *all* 'bodies' (male, female, child) were perceived
exclusively as sources of *labour*.

The belated gendering of historiography is reflected in wider
literary and cultural debates where, as in many independence
movements globally, nationalist struggles were assumed to be
'gender-free'. It is not surprising then that the writers widely
recognized as inaugurating 'Caribbean Literature' in the 1940s
and 1950s were male: V. S. Naipaul, Samuel Selvon, George
Lamming, Wilson Harris, Derek Walcott, Kamau Brathwaite, to
name a few. This generation of writers had a colonial education
which would have involved being 'drilled' in the appreciation of
English literature, learning to memorize ('learn by heart')
particular canonical texts to perform in class or in one of the
many elocution competitions staged across the Caribbean. These
performances might be read as enacting one of the many
paradoxes of colonialism: 'the native' is declared 'uncivilized'
but simultaneously must be stripped of his culture. As Franz
Fanon argues, 'By a kind of perverted logic, it [colonialism] turns
to the past of the oppressed, and distorts, disfigures and
destroys it.'[5] In a context where the aspiring West Indian
writer's right to write was so profoundly questioned, it is 'a
mystery', George Lamming argues, that so many writers *did*, 'the
historical fact is that this "emergence" of a dozen or so novelists
in the British Caribbean with some fifty books to their credit or

disgrace, and all published between 1948 and 1958, is in the nature of a phenomenon.'[6] That this historical context would generate highly charged debates about appropriate style, voice and subject matter is not surprising. Lamming saw the West Indian writer as providing a crucial role in relation to the wider population, 'It is the West Indian novel that has restored the peasant to his true and original status of personality.'[7] V. S. Naipaul was more pessimistic: 'Living in a borrowed culture, the West Indian, more than most, needs writers to tell him who he is and where he stands. Here the West Indian writers have failed. Most have so far only reflected and flattered the prejudices of their race or colour groups.'[8] Some years later, with different emphasis, Derek Walcott in 'The Muse of History', reiterated Naipaul's view: 'In the New World servitude to the muse of history has produced a literature of recrimination and despair, a literature of revenge written by the descendants of slaves or a literature of remorse written by the descendants of masters.'[9]

The combative tone characterizing the reception of early West Indian writing, became polarized around a European/African binary in which the former represented the elitism of Eurocentric culture and the latter a more appropriately populist Afrocentricism. Debates about what constituted an authentic West Indian literary voice became particularly heated in relation to poetry where the use of Caribbean Creole as well as African-American vernacular idioms was increasingly perceived as most effective in challenging poetic orthodoxies and the decorum of Standard English (hereafter SE). Not everyone supported this view; Eric Roach responded to a special edition of the journal *Savacou: New Writing* published in 1971 which included many experiments with black American and West Indian Creole speech and rhythms by asking, 'Are we going to tie the drum of Africa to our tails and bay like mad dogs at the Nordic world to which our geography and history tie us?'[10] Roach's description of the tussle over poetic registers as a battle between 'Afro-Saxons and tribe boys'[11] conveys a sense of the combativeness of these debates. A short extract from 'Mabrak' (by Bongo Jerry) conveys the tenor of combative machismo that characterized this cultural moment:

5

MAN must use MEN language
to carry dis message:
SILENCE BABEL TONGUES; recall and
recollect BLACK SPEECH.[12]

The capitalized words here consolidate the sense that the man-speaker SHOUTS his message. This vocal register of protest has tended to remain the dominant one as Caribbean critical discourses continue to emphasize the local and the popular (reggae, dub and, more recently, dancehall) as distinctively Caribbean cultural expressions.

In her poem 'Shell Blow' Senior offers a wry commentary on Caribbean literary history. A beached shell promises to provide not the romance of 'ocean song' but the blast of history, 'the real thing, a blast-out, everybody's/ history' (*Shell*: 33). While Caribbean people may be masters of mixing, dubbing and splicing, the speaker argues, 'we still can't find/ a way to erase not one word.' (*Shell*: 34) Rather than denying or ignoring 'the deep amnesiac blow' of history, as Walcott describes it in 'Laventille',[13] the speaker urges a return to the multiplicity of stories – big and small – that comprise history via 'shell blow'. Senior welds the traditional use of the conch shell as instrument of communication (to announce births, deaths, meetings, warnings, uprisings) to modern technologies of print and recording – 'every whorl a book of life,/ a text, a motion picture, a recording' (*Shell*: 33). By implication, the shell also stands in for the poet who calls to 'People/ no longer hearing, not wanting to listen/ over the noise coming in.' (*Shell*: 35), people who, suspended in an eternal present tense – 'marking time' (*Shell*: 38) – are:

> Convinced their name is Nobody,
> born in a place that is called Nothing, for
> it is Historyless. For History is invention
> and nothing invent yaso according to
> Famous Author that was the last
> I was to hear about before all over
> The Caribbean shell by any name stop blow:
>
> (*Shell*: 38–9)

In *The Middle Passage* Naipaul famously argued that 'History is built around achievement and creation; and nothing was

6

created in the West Indies.'[14] Senior ponders on the enduring impact of this '"nothing/nothing" mantra' (*Shell*: 39) and posits the passing on of *stories* – big and small – as a necessary corrective. Again in 'Shell Blow', Senior invokes the words of another 'Famous Author', Edward Kamau Brathwaite. His poem, 'Calypso', from his pioneering *The Arrivants: A New World Trilogy*, opens:

> The stone had skidded arc'd and bloomed into islands:
> Cuba and San Domingo
> Jamaica and Puerto Rico
> Grenada Guadeloupe Bonaire[15]

In Senior's poem, the speaker envisages the skipping stone which Brathwaite uses as metaphor for the Caribbean archipelago 'sinking into itself,/ into *nada*' unless we 'Pop "tory" and "PASS IT ON"' (*Shell*: 39–40). The poem takes stock of Caribbean literary history as it negotiates between the impasse of Naipaul's 'nothing' and the suspended possibilities of Brathwaite's skipping stone. Senior presents history as a dynamic process, a chain of stories to be repeated, revised and relayed and the poet as a figure caught up in that process rather than commentating from a position outside it. I argue that Senior's approach here might be interpreted as an intervention that quietly and wryly disrupts the combatively male trajectory sketched above.

## 'WOMAN' IN/AND CARIBBEAN WRITING

Senior is one of many women writers and critics who have contributed to the process of assessing and revising Caribbean literary history as it came to be defined in the 1970s. As the disappointments of the post-independence era set in, cultural nationalist positions became harder to uphold and the remit of Caribbean Literature more uncertain. The interventions of women writers and critics became more visible as global feminist movements grew and challenged nationalist orthodoxies. Women *had* been writing during the 'first wave' of Caribbean publications (Una Marson and Phyllis Shand Allfrey among many others) but, with very few exceptions, had received little attention.[16] Notable among these belatedly recognized writers is Louise Bennett, one of the few women

7

poets writing and performing her work from the mid-1940s onwards. Arguably, it wasn't until the publication of Bennett's *Selected Poems* in 1982, edited and with a scholarly introduction by Mervyn Morris, that her work really began to be taken seriously by the literary establishment. Bennett's profound impact on Caribbean literary culture, particularly with regard to establishing a Creole literary voice, is widely recognized. J. E. Chamberlin in his study of Caribbean poetry, *Come Back to Me My Language* claims, 'More than any other single writer, Louise Bennett brought local language into the foreground of West Indian cultural life'.[17] While Paula Burnett, in her introduction to *The Penguin Book of Caribbean Verse in English* argues: 'By fortuitous circumstances in 1943, a 24-year-old Jamaican lady, Louise Bennett, was allowed to read a few of her dialect poems on Jamaica's first radio station. The event launched a people's voice.'[18]

Olive Senior, too, recognizes Bennett's impact: 'all of us, I think, have been influenced by Louise Bennett, who was a pioneer in writing Creole and speaking it – because it was something revolutionary.'[19] Where initially Bennett's promotion of Jamaican Creole (hereafter JC) was seen primarily as a 'folk-culture' phenomenon and not part of prestigious literary debates, this perception has been dramatically adjusted, if not reversed. Her recognition of the creative potential of JC and her deployment of it in a sustained way over many decades has been crucial in establishing Caribbean Creole as a rich literary resource in its own right and a powerful alternative to the received notions of literary form and voice.

Bennett's speakers are frequently African-Jamaican women, usually working-class and always Creole-speaking. Her preferred linguistic register is 'labrish' (JC for gossip) as indicated in the title of her first collection, *Jamaica Labrish: Jamaica Dialect Poems* (1966). Punning, tracing, cursing or showing off, Bennett skilfully demonstrated the flexibility and performative power of JC in poems in which the poet stayed 'in role', seldom self-consciously drawing attention to the control of the poet in producing her personae. Bennett died in 2006 and in a special issue of the *Journal of West Indian Writing* dedicated to her work, Ifeoma Kiddoe Nwankwo describes Bennett as 'without a doubt Jamaica's definitive national poet'.[20] Her poems are often performed by Jamaican school children, a development which attests to the power of her work as a vehicle for national pride but also as a manoeuvre which displaces canonical English texts as the preferred choice for 'learning by heart'. Bennett has influenced a range of writers in the wider Caribbean and its diaspora and across gender and generation, from John Agard and Jean Binta Breeze in Britain to Lillian Allen and Olive Senior in Canada. Some have followed the trajectory of more-or-less exclusive use of Caribbean Creole in performative modes of labrish, dub, protest, and social commentary (Valerie Bloom, Jean Binta Breeze, John Agard, Lillian Allen, Mutabaruka, Linton Kwesi Johnson, among others). Others, like Senior, have made more economic, modulated use of Caribbean Creole, finding in Bennett's work a reservoir of folk voices from which to take fragments that can be embedded alongside Standard English on the page.

Bennett's influence is perhaps more immediately apparent in Senior's short stories in the deployment of Jamaican Creole-speaking narrators and in the extensive use of JC in the dialogues that are so central to Senior's stories. Like Bennett, Senior's stories draw attention to the pithy expressiveness of JC and to the cultural values it encodes. And, like Louise Bennett, Olive Senior has also invested considerable energy in collating Jamaican folk culture. But where Bennett's JC-speakers are expansive, physically expressive and voluble, Senior's also include JC-speakers who are reflective and understated. Her oeuvre is indebted to but also extends Bennett's use of JC from a largely public declamatory mode where social critique and humour are paramount to include more private, internal musings and a more nuanced range of registers. This distinction is most evident in the poetry where Senior only occasionally makes sustained use of JC, often opting to signal a Creole speaker by a handful of JC codes. Where in her stories, Senior provides naturalistic representations of JC, deploying recognizably African-Jamaican speakers, the poems make more strategic use of JC and deploy speakers whose identities are more mutable and ethnically varied, mediated as they are through an Anansi-like poetic consciousness which is lightly punning and cunning.

9

Anansi, the shape-shifting trickster spider-figure originating in West African culture, is a familiar figure in folklore across the Caribbean where his skill in outwitting opponents of superior strength is admired almost as much as is his greed and selfishness. Anansi's particular abilities to cunningly 'tek bad things mek good' is powerfully resonant for Caribbean subjects, given the violent history sketched above. *Appearing* to be docile and acquiescent was a crucial strategy for survival on the plantations; as the Guyanese poet, Grace Nichols puts it in her cycle of poems on enslaved women, *i is a long memoried woman*, 'Not every skin teeth is a smile massa'.[21] Strategies of dissembling and shape-shifting, developed on the plantation, continue to inform cultural practices and critical vocabularies in the Americas.[22] Some would argue that Caribbean women, given the contradictory nature of their roles, have had particular reasons to deploy Anansi-style tactics. As Senior outlines in *Working Miracles*, many of the women she interviewed (across class categories) reported the need to disguise any power they *did* have to avoid alienating their male partners. Louise Bennett's poem, 'Jamaica Oman' treats this dynamic wittily by praising the Jamaican woman's cunning, 'Look how long dem liberated/ an de man dem never know!'; the poem continues:

> Neck an neck an foot an foot wid man
> she buckle hole her own;
> While man a call her 'so-so rib'
> Oman a tun backbone![23]

Bennett's celebration of the *covert* expression of female power was taken up by the editors of Jamaica's first 'woman-only' anthology of poetry in the title chosen, *Jamaica Woman*. The poems reflect on diverse aspects of postcolonial Jamaican life, often from an explicitly feminist position but it is indicative of the suspicion surrounding 'feminism' that the editors in their preface reassure the reader that, 'There is nothing limp in the responses of the poets here, nor is there any aggressive feminism in their work'.[24] This careful equivocation may well attest to the suspicion surrounding feminism as 'a foreign Western import' but it perhaps also indicates sensitivity about articulating a distinctly female perspective in the context of post-independence Jamaica where harsh economic realities

10

impact forcefully on women *and* men and where arguments that women's relative empowerment risks emasculating men (the 'men-in-crisis' argument) continue to have currency. Certainly it implies that the would-be-feminist Caribbean woman must negotiate her feminism carefully, tightrope walking between the more overtly articulated feminism associated with movements in Europe and North America in the 1970s and 1980s and local realities and 'womanist' histories.

Despite initial reservations about embracing 'feminist' as a designated category, most commentators acknowledge that the sheer number of Caribbean women's texts being published in the 1980s is one of the striking features of that decade of literary activity – something 'in the nature of a phenomenon' to match that of the male writers of the 1950s. By the 1990s Caribbean women's writing was well established as a distinct field of writing, supported by interest from publishers as well as by the paraphernalia of scholarly interest (university syllabi, conferences and academic journal publications). Olive Senior is a central figure in these developments, along with Erna Brodber, Lorna Goodison, Grace Nichols, Jamaica Kincaid, Dionne Brand, Merle Hodge and Sylvia Wynter and many others. These writers' texts might loosely be described as woman-centred, with recurring themes including: mother/daughter relationships; child-bearing and rearing; the restrictive and constrictive socialization of girls; sexuality and the female body; as well as an overarching concern with colonial and national patriarchies. The particular form and focus of this emphasis was varied: the noisy Creole poetics of Merle Hodge in *Crick Crack Monkey*; the *jouissance* of Erna Brodber's *Jane and Louisa Will Soon Come Home*; the cleanly articulated rage of Jamaica Kincaid's *Annie John*; the playful sexual poetics of Grace Nichols' *The Fat Black Woman's Poems*. Olive Senior shares many of these concerns: her short stories, for example, share the focus on gender socialization, particularly of girls, and her work engages repeatedly with the debilitating legacy of colonialism. But her work also brings a quieter and more subversively cunning register to this textual mix, as the following chapters will argue.

Like the earlier male writers, Caribbean women writers responded to the distortions of selfhood generated by colonial structures. In Senior's, 'Colonial Girls School', the speaker

11

catalogues the alignments with European and North American history, geography and literature that the girls were expected to make while learning nothing about Marcus Garvey, the black civil rights movement, African anti-colonial struggles or African Jamaican cultural forms – or *themselves*. The repeated refrain of the poem, 'Told us nothing about ourselves/ There was nothing about us at all', emphasizes the systematic nature of this process of denial:

> Borrowed images
> willed our skin pale
> muffled our laughter
> lowered our voices
> let out our hems
> dekinked our hair
> denied our sex in gym tunics and bloomers
> harnessed our voices to madrigals
> and genteel airs
> yoked our minds to declensions in Latin
> and the language of Shakespeare
> Told us nothing about ourselves
> There was nothing about us at all

(*TT*: 26)

It also foregrounds the disciplining of the black (and/or 'non-white') girl-child's *body* into a more acceptably decorous version of femininity. When male writers, influenced by the negritude movement, wrote poems that conflated black women with the land and with the fruits of the land, few Caribbean women were persuaded. So over-determined is this sexualization of the black female body that many critics suggest it is unsurprising that some Caribbean women writers have avoided representing the body at all. This may also account for the fact that Olive Senior has tended to dwell on the female body in its 'becoming' or 'in-between' stage, rather than on the adult woman's body.

But even as Caribbean women's writing was consolidating itself as a field of study in the late 1990s, tensions appeared centred largely on the tendency to assume 'the' Caribbean woman was African Caribbean, working-class and heterosexual. These assumptions had been made about 'the' Caribbean man in the earlier male works, despite the foregrounding of Indian Caribbean realities by Naipaul and Selvon. It is also the case that

12

by the late 1990s, feminism as a global movement could no longer assume solidarity between women, across differences. These proliferating fractures, while they undermined the category 'Caribbean women's writing', have opened up spaces for more diverse configurations of feminist work, particularly in relation to questions of ethnicity and sexuality. There is now a growing body of work on Indian Caribbean writers and some work on Chinese and Portuguese women's writing. Brinda Mehta, following Rosanne Kanhai and Shalini Puri's arguments (who, in turn, build on Torabully's idea of 'coolitude' as a parallel to 'negritude') makes the case for 'dougla poetics'[25] as a paradigm that might allow for fuller recognition of Indian contributions to Caribbean culture.[26] But while this renders Indian subjects visible/audible, it clearly elides others (Amerindian, Chinese, Portuguese, Lebanese as well as other 'mixed race' categories) and follows the tendency established in Creolization models of privileging certain aspects of 'the mix' as distinct aggregates so that 'hybridity' is in effect the sum of its parts rather than a 'new' and distinct cultural formation. Here, I would argue that Senior has persistently refused to privilege any particular ethnicity in her work but has patiently worked at embedding references to a diverse range of Caribbean cultures. Creole and hybrid cultures in her work tend to offer more complicated and ambiguous possibilities, as the discussions in the following chapters will show.

The tussle over the foundational 'component' of Creole culture continues today and has its loudest voicing in the controversy centred on homophobia in popular cultural forms, particularly in Jamaica dancehall. Creole forms such as carnival, calypso and Anansi stories have informed literary culture in varying degrees from the 1950s, often consolidated around Louise Bennett's work. But from the 1990s, emphasis has shifted as other Creole forms, such as reggae, ragga and dancehall have gained prominence within the region and its diaspora. In *Sound Clash: Jamaican Dancehall Culture at Large* (2004), Carolyn Cooper argues that the spectacularly loud, irreverent display of heterosexual sexuality central to dancehall culture (which she sees as a strong component of African Jamaican Creole forms), along with the 'slack'/ sexually explicit lyrics of dancehall DJs, provides a necessarily robust expression of agency for disempowered,

13

black. working-class Jamaican men. By contrast, feminist and queer theorists/activists argue that the violent misogyny and homophobia in ragga lyrics endorses violence towards both gays and women and indeed, *incites* it against gay men in particular. Activists in the UK and North America organized their outrage at dancehall lyrics so powerfully that certain performers have been banned from performing in Britain and North America.[27] Unsurprisingly, this generated outraged responses, in turn, from Jamaicans who perceived it as yet another form of cultural imperialism.

The Caribbean remains economically and culturally vulnerable with high unemployment rates forcing reliance on the service industry and on remittances from Caribbeans living abroad. Honor Ford-Smith suggests that lack of job opportunities at home, makes Jamaica 'an impoverished holding area for labour that it is unable to employ', forcing migration in unfavourable, piecemeal conditions.[28] In this context, narratives of 'men-in-crisis' and an emasculation of culture continue to generate the perceived need for a robust and loudly vocal combative cultural response. But, as well as reproducing the mistaken assumption that women are not part of the labour force affected, a normatively male, and aggressively combative politics may also short-circuit other registers and modes of protest. As Honor Ford-Smith argues, it creates an ethos in which hyper-masculinity becomes unavoidable:

> My point is simply that when glamourised images of armoured masculinity are the dominant images in circulation in a context of extreme inequity, they naturalize and normalise violent relationships and create notions of style, taste, pleasure and possibility that become linked to them, contributing to their reproduction.[29]

Endorsing dancehall and other aggressively male forms of Creole culture as the privileged repository of a grittily authentic Creole culture drowns out quieter registers of Creole expression and less combative modes of resisting, such as Senior's. It also presents the encounter between 'the local' and 'the global' in unnecessarily oppositional terms: a 'defensive cultural nationalism' versus a powerfully vocal 'metropolitan liberalism' generates an unproductive stand-off between local and global cultural forces, overly dramatizing the tussle over what

Caribbean culture signifies within the region as well as globally.[30] It has also confirmed a view of the Caribbean (and Jamaica in particular) as not only 'the most homophobic place on earth' but as a hyper-sexualized space of loud, flamboyant *spectacle*; indeed there is a well-documented history of sex-tourism in Jamaica. This elides the more contradictory and nuanced realities that prevail in a culture where sexual 'slackness' exists alongside a deeply conservative sexual politics. Indeed the justifications for anti-gay attitudes are put forward by 'upstanding' pastors and other establishment figures as often as they are encoded in dancehall lyrics. Senior's work, I suggest, is alert to these contradictions, offering a critique of conservative notions of 'respectability' as well as suggesting how 'respectability' might be deployed strategically as another, quieter register of resistance.

The aggressive refusal of the homosexual and homoerotic in dancehall perhaps also clearly undermines another popular representation, that of the Caribbean as a space of cultural plurality, the accommodation of difference and a kind of happy-go-lucky mobility – a 'happy hybridity', if you will. James Clifford famously proclaimed, 'We are all Caribbeans now...in our urban archipelagos',[31] implying that the migration and flux which characterize contemporary global realities (and the hybrid identities that result from multiple crossings) has its most emphatic moorings in the Caribbean. But the contemporary reality for Jamaica and many parts of the postcolonial Caribbean involves a much more tense idea of hybridity than this. Senior's work frequently reminds us of this as it explores and exposes the contradictory meanings of Creole hybridity.

Olive Senior's writing, across several genres and more than three decades, allows useful interventions into and interruptions of these literary histories and their attendant orthodoxies. Many of her poems and short stories explore the ongoing impact of a rigid colonial racial hierarchy in which 'light skin' and 'good hair', if carefully nurtured, can ensure upward social mobility. Her work is populated by characters seeking to deny or enhance aspects of their ethnicity in ways that fracture family and community and unsettle ideas of any easy embrace of hybridity, exposing the painful personal choices and consequences that result from deeply ingrained attitudes to race. In 'Cockpit

Country Dreams', a mother advises her child to be selective about her ancestry:

> Listen child, said my mother
> whose hands plundered photo albums
> of all black ancestors: Herein
> your ancestry, your imagery, your pride.
> Choose *this* river, *this* rhythm, *this* road.
> Walk good in the footsteps of *these* fathers.
>
> (*TT*: 4)

The daughter rejects this advice and instead embraces, not without some ambivalence, the uncertainty generated by embracing the multiple strands of her ancestry:

> Now my disorder of ancestry
> proves as stable as the many rivers
> flowing around me. Undocumented
> I drown in the other's history
>
> (*TT*: 5)

The ambiguities and complications involved in this 'disorder of ancestry' inflect the tenor of Senior's handling of 'race' throughout her oeuvre. Her own background is varied and she describes her parents as 'mixed': black, British, and, on her father's side some Jewish ancestry, she says in a recent interview, 'I say I'm Heinz 57 varieties because I think I'm a mixture of a whole lot of things but I can't say I'm a quarter this or a half this.'[32] Although Senior grew up in the isolated, deeply rural context of Cockpit Country in Trelawny, from a young age she was sent to stay with relatively well-off relations and went to school in the towns of Troy and then Hanover. This shuttling between town and country also exposed Senior to diverse cultures with regard to class and race in ways that impacted profoundly on her sensibility as a writer. She reflects on this in an interview: 'The constant tug between private aloofness and community and social sharing has shaped my personality, my world-view and my work. So too have the contradictions inherent in race and class, in poverty and wealth, power and powerlessness, European values versus indigenous values rooted in Africa.'[33] The polarized dimensions foregrounded here suggest a more tense and anxious negotiation of 'raced' identity than the more playful possibilities conventionally

16

aligned with creolization processes. Taken as a whole, Senior's work critiques, endorses and patiently extends the possibilities for creolization. It ranges widely across cultural worlds to inscribe not just African and European cultural forms but to insist on retrieving and exploring traces of Amerindian presences (and absences) as well as other marginalized groups within the Caribbean. Senior's use of genre is interesting in this regard for the distinct modes of writing she deploys all contribute cumulatively to this project, conveying a subtle understanding of Caribbean realities past and present: many of the short stories offer portraits of rural and urban Jamaican communities which expose the prejudices, difficulties and pleasures of life in Jamaica from the mid-twentieth century onwards. In the poems fragments of the past are often excavated painstakingly to contribute to detailed, small-scale re-constructions (and revisions) of Caribbean history. And the collation of cultural forms in the archival works function as a dispassionate and broad catalogue of the many cultures that have impacted on the Caribbean. Together these works provide access to the multiple and diverse components of *latent* Jamaican and Caribbean creolization possibilities, even if Senior's wry, wary perspective recognizes that a full delivery of this Creole hybridity is not-yet-possible, given the violent genesis of the region:

> What can I say? The fragmentation of the Caribbean was historically determined by European penetration and conquest – and we have never managed to transcend these boundaries. [...] Despite all the rhetoric about Caribbean economic integration, a new centre-periphery system is evolving which is based in Washington and a new cultural system is evolving located somewhere between Dallas and Hollywood.[34]

But alongside this idea of fragmented, economically and culturally vulnerable nation states, Senior also suggests a more enabling way of viewing fragmentation: 'In the Caribbean I think we're special because we haven't inherited a past that can be traced in a well-ordered, linear kind of way, we represent the coming together of fragments of people bringing fragments of their cultures with them and these fragments have coalesced over time into something that's kaleidoscopic.'[35] One of Senior's great strengths is to be able in her fiction, poetry and non-fiction to offer detailed insights into the varied fragments that comprise Caribbean culture while still investing in a sense of the region's culture as a – fragile – whole. Her work refuses to present any easy or celebratory narrative about creolization or unity-in-diversity but instead worries away at the detail of the small stories, the individual lives and the particularities of her/their/ our lived landscapes to illuminate those fragments.

# 2

# The Story as Gossip: Creolizing the Text

> I would say 'home' is a place where there is a condition of
> resonance, or sound returned; that is, a place where you
> speak to a community and it speaks back to you.[1]

Senior gained international attention in 1987 when she won the
inaugural Commonwealth Writer's Prize for *Summer Lightning
and Other Stories* (1986). Reviewers praised the liveliness and
authenticity of her representation of rural Jamaican communities, particularly the accuracy with which Jamaican Creole
speech was rendered and the compelling manner of her
representation of the anxieties, concerns and pleasures of
children within these overlooked and 'marginal' communities.
The two collections of stories that followed, *The Arrival of the
Snake Woman and Other Stories* (1989) and *Discerner of Hearts and
Other Stories* (1995), consolidated Senior's reputation as a short-
story writer with these distinct strengths.

The 'home' provides Senior with the subject matter of many
of her short stories, most of which are set in the relatively tightly
delineated socio-cultural space of rural Jamaica from the 1940s
onwards, documenting the everyday realities of 'ordinary'
country folk as well as commenting on the forces that impact
on these communities to unsettle and change them. In some
stories, this sense of tightly circumscribed space is emphasized
by being set in the geographically isolated location of Cockpit
Country, Senior's childhood home. Girl-children populate these
stories as protagonists and/or narrators who operate in diverse
ways: sometimes as figures who can interpret and respond to
change more flexibly than adults around them and at others as
repositories of the hopes and expectations of parental figures

and the community at large. The family is presented as a fluid and protean concept and children often appear to belong to the community at large. 'Family' and 'community' are represented as structures that provide support for children, in noisy, unpredictable and generous ways. But they are also acknowledged as structures that discipline children harshly into regimes of respectability shaped by religious conformity and hypocritical moral codes. Racial hierarchies established under the plantocracy when mapped onto the class structures of the postcolonial Caribbean, continue to privilege those with 'lighter skins' so that 'success' appears to be their exclusive prerogative. Senior's stories explore the anxiety this produces in children when parental figures seek to socialize them into better-off 'whiter' futures. In *Working Miracles* Senior argues that: 'individuals often teeter between two or more racial and cultural ideals: on the one hand the received white European culture of these territories, on the other the culture based on blood and ethnic origins – especially African or Indian – which has been partly or largely "submerged". The result for many is severe cultural imbalance' (*WM*: 26–7).

In the prevailing context of the economic impoverishment that shapes the lives of Senior's subjects, opportunities for social advancement are precious and few, and children who are perceived as having natural attributes that might allow them to be groomed for a better life ('clear skin', 'good hair', for example) are often shifted to relatives, however distant, who are better equipped to oversee the child's upward social mobility. This process, with its emphasis on physiognomy has particular implications for girl-children and the stories repeatedly expose the repressive practices deemed necessary to discipline girls into respectable norms of femininity in appearance (straightening hair, softening skin to keep it 'clear', speaking 'properly' and so on) and in behaviour (demure and modest to avoid the 'fall' that pregnancy represents). *All* girls, the stories imply, are haunted by the spectre of pregnancy which threatens to 'undo' whatever upward social mobility they can achieve by careful management of their 'feminine assets'. Paradoxically, these harsh regimes of gender socialization exist alongside a widely held view that children signify woman's most enduring value to the society.

Many of the stories concern children who, in one way or another, are orphaned or live away from their biological parent(s). Sometimes Senior deploys vulnerable children to expose the ambitions of adults; at others the ignored child becomes a 'secret agent' of sorts, quietly observing and interpreting the world around her as the adults continue their manoeuvres. In the process she reveals tensions within these communities between a pressure to 'fit in' with the community's ethos and to escape it by 'doing better'. This is reflected at a wider level in the way the stories oscillate between nostalgia for an old order associated with a rural Jamaican-Creole culture that is complexly humane with diverse rituals and courtesies, alongside a recognition of the limitations and prejudices that make leaving desirable – and necessary. Senior evokes a cast of characters whose stories, riddles and gossip are powerfully expressive despite the harsh realities of their lives. The impact of migration on the lives and culture of those left behind as well as on those who leave is a recurring thread in these narratives, implying success and failure in varying measure. As the epigraph of this chapter indicates, 'community' provides Senior with her subject matter but community also influences the form her writing takes with its emphasis on a dynamic interchange between writer/reader and speaker/listener and a sense of the written being 'aerated' by the oral. This chapter discusses the sense of community that Senior's stories inscribe and the literary voice that both produces and is produced by this sense of community.

## STORY (AS) *TELLING*

In her essay entitled, 'The Poem as Gardening, the Story as Su-su: Finding a Literary Voice' Senior emphasizes the impact of story-telling traditions in the rural context of her childhood: 'As a writer, I consider myself a gossip in this sense, the god-parent of the story or poem that enters the world, announcing, "I have something to tell you"' (Senior, 'The Poem as Gardening', 2005: 46–7).[2] The oral quality of Senior's stories is immediately evident in the prevalence and variety of Creole speech usage, whether in the form of direct speech, the use of Creole narrators or

21

occasional Creole phrases. It is also evident in a range of devices associated with traditions of oral story telling which together suggest ways that the written short story is here inflected powerfully by the oral to produce what Hyacinth Simpson calls an 'oral poetics'. Three stories from *Summer Lightning* establish this sense of orality clearly. In 'Do Angels Wear Brassieres?', Senior has her feisty protagonist, Beccka, challenge the visiting Archdeacon by using a series of riddles in order to 'test' this eminent visitor to her aunt's house. Riddles, a traditional feature of oral forms, invite the listener to participate in solving a puzzle in a manner similar to that of the call and response. Beccka prepares for this challenge by closely reading her Bible, recognizing the authority invested in this text which is quoted frequently in her community. The story is narrated in JC and in a register that is similar to the many adult conversations that Beccka eavesdrops on (particularly the gossip of self-righteous Auntie Mary and her nosey neighbour Katie) so that as readers we 'overhear' much of the background to the story. We hear that Beccka and her mother Cherry have been accommodated by Auntie Mary after being abandoned by Beccka's father, a married man, who has abandoned both his 'inside' ('legitimate') *and* 'outside' ('illegitimate') families and gone abroad. Importantly, Beccka's father's love of books is interpreted by the two women as the main reason for his dereliction as well as an explanation for Beccka's impudent curiosity, 'Book is all him ever good for. Rather than buy food put in the pickney mouth or help Cherry find shelter his only contribution is book. Nuh his character stamp on her.' (*SL*: 69) Thus, although Beccka is presented as well-versed in the art of orality, her character is also shaped in important ways by 'book culture', characterized here as alien to the community *and* distinct from that other 'Book', the Bible, declaimed extracts of which punctuate every-day life in the Caribbean.

The last riddling question Beccka poses to the Archdeacon when he finally deigns to visit their home for tea, 'do angels wear brassieres?' gives the story its title and provides the comic focus: Mary stops in horror at the child's impudent question, collides with Cherry and upsets the elaborate tea-tray. Mary is mortified, the Archdeacon relieved not to have to answer Beccka's question and Cherry responds by throwing a kitchen cloth over her head and bawling. Senior carefully orchestrates the denouement for maximum comic effect.[3] Through comedy, and the disruption caused by Beccka's disingenuously practical question, 'respectability' is disrupted spectacularly. The carnivalesque potential of Creole performativity is deployed as a tool here to expose aspirations to middle-class respectability. But Senior also suggests that Beccka's feistiness is generated by an ability to effectively manipulate *both* oral and written traditions and to make discerning interpretive choices between them. She backs up her instinctive mistrust of her aunt and the Archdeacon by deploying *reasoning* strategies that are associated with the conventions of oral performances *and* by reading and reflection. The story ends with Beccka anticipating a bigger role as provocateur when she starts at one of the best schools on the island, implying that she will continue to act as a disrupting, if not carnivalesque force in that establishment too.

'Real Old Time T'ing' also deploys an omniscient Creole-speaking narrator who interpellates the reader as a listener already familiar with the community and its values. We are introduced to one of the story's significant figures by being offered a complex genealogy which we are expected to follow: 'Miss Myrtella is Papa Sterling cousin, far remove, bout third cousin. Mek me see, Papa Sterling grandfather Mass Jake did have a daughter on the side with a Fletcher woman name Addie.' (SL: 57) The narrative is also peppered with rhetorical questions and exhortations with which the reader/listener is expected to agree. The first sentence immerses the reader into the story without any preamble: 'Is the one name Patricia did start up bout how Papa Sterling need a new house for it look bad how their father living in this old board house it don't even have sanitary convenience. Sanitary convenience! So it don't name bath house no more?' (SL: 54) The issue of naming is developed into a wider contestation over language, meaning and value as the story progresses. Patricia's attempts to get her father to upgrade his house is evidently less motivated by concern for his well-being than by her desire for her own economic success to be made *visible* to the villagers. Papa Stirling is teased about all the 'modern' equipment and excess of rooms this upgraded house will have: '"Gwine have kitchen with real real sink. Bathroom with real real bath. Bedroom with real real bed."/ "*An*

23

*living room with real real living"*, the boys dem all shout out.' (*SL*: 56) The repetition of 'real' is clearly comedic; the mockery in the line the boys all chorus about a living room 'with real real living', suggesting a critique of the fakery involved in this staged, self-consciously 'modern' way of living. But there is also an undercurrent of unease about a comfortable reality that *does* exist elsewhere and that desires for such comforts must, of necessity, be repressed if the equilibrium of the village is to be maintained. These complications are not expressed by the narrator who, like the villagers, takes Papa Sterling's side against his status-hungry daughter, indicating her relish with frequent interjections, 'see here' (*SL*: 57), 'This is just the start' (*SL*: 59), 'And hear this! Now I come to the best part of everything.' (*SL*: 65)

The directness of narration is presented as a refreshingly frank contrast to the deviousness of Patricia whose pretentiousness is rendered even more comic by the fact that her modern lifestyle also includes a desire to find 'her roots' by acquiring as many items of old furniture, crockery and ornaments as she can from the villagers, who she feels don't appreciate the *true* value of these items. They crave plastic chairs and aluminium dinette sets, cheaper modern consumer goods which they can afford. The narrator recognizes Patricia's quest for 'roots' as acquisitive and as a need to signal just how *far* she has moved from her rural childhood 'roots' despite, in literal terms, only migrating as far as Kingston. The fact that the antiques she most covets belong to Myrtella and are of colonial English provenance compounds the irony of Patricia's quest for 'roots'. Myrtella refuses to sell them because she *does* recognize their 'real' 'ancestral' value as items passed on from her mother's mother. The story ends with the villagers embracing Papa Sterling's marriage to Myrtella for despite her residence in England and her 'speaky-spoky ways' (*SL*: 63) she is genuine, 'real', in ways that Patricia is not, and her values less materialistic. Senior presents the narrator and the community as one able through gossip, folk wisdom and bantering conversations to weigh up with interpretive acuity the values of those hustling up the social ladder. The image of Myrtella's 'ole time t'ings' (a coronation mug, claw-foot umbrella rack etc) relocated in Papa Sterling's humble abode also suggests a kind of hybrid dwelling-place that is perhaps 'modern' in its own low-key, creolized way.

'Ascot' also opens in the middle of a conversation and is punctuated throughout with direct appeals to the reader/ listener ('See here!' 'well sah', 'See ya pappyshow' and so on). The eponymous, 'Ascot', an ungainly man with uncommonly big feet, is known in the village variously as a charmer, a fool or a scoundrel, the degree of affection being dictated by the extent to which an individual has been affected by Ascot's trickery and petty thieving. Where Mama thinks Ascot's cunning will take him far (as indeed it does when he 'loses' himself illegally in the USA), Papa, who lost a bunch of his prized bananas to Ascot's greed, thinks prison is his likely destination. The story is narrated by their daughter Lily, who listens to these conversations and in the process of telling the story, negotiates her own opinion as she ponders the various responses to Ascot. The comic denouement in this story comes when Ascot returns from New York to visit, driving a big car, dressed in white from head-to-toe and accompanied by an American wife with an MA. If in 'Real Old Time T'ing' Patricia wants to beautify her past in line with her aspirations to a middle-class lifestyle, in this story Ascot seeks to *deny* his past by refusing to recognize his mother and instead attaching himself to the narrator's family because they are better off. This is where Lily draws a clear moral line, refusing to be swayed either by the indulgence of the women, including her mother, who are charmed by Ascot or by the filial pride that Ascot's mother takes in his achievements despite her son's denial of her. In this sense the narration offers its own paradigm of interpretation, a hermeneutics-on-the-hoof, as it were, via Lily's weighing-up of positions in the process of telling the story. Hyacinth Simpson argues persuasively that Ascot is based on the Jamaican trickster figure 'Big Boy' (a figure who succeeds despite being stupid and without morals) and that Senior deploys this figure effectively to raise questions about the extent to which the transgression of societal mores can or should be tolerated.[4] Rather than being static, Senior's stories imply that folk traditions are mutable and enriching forms that have ongoing relevance for rural Jamaicans.

The stories discussed so far are energetically comedic in their use of Creole as a force capable of disrupting respectability and undermining pretensions, a use that follows on from that established by Louise Bennett. Senior notes that: 'Louise Bennett was a high school graduate, and yet she dared to get up and talk in Creole. Now, when I was a child we all learned Louise Bennett poems, but we did them, like, at school concerts so that people would laugh. It still was not accepted – in other words it was something you laughed at.'[5] In the discussion of the four stories that follows, I argue that Senior seeks to extend and nuance the representation of Creole speech and culture in significant ways beyond the comedic. In the quote above, it is the perceived *gap* between Bennett's educated status and the supposedly 'uneducated' Creole speakers she impersonates that generates the humour. There is also a sense in which the performance of Creole speech hinges on larger-than-life qualities, high volume and spectacular display. Senior deploys child narrators and protagonists to explore more ambivalent explorations of Creole speech and culture.

## CHILDHOOD AND CHILD SUBJECTS

Children feature prominently in the stories discussed so far as provocateurs, catalysts for change, and as observers and facilitators. But Senior also focuses on children in ways that expose and reflect on their vulnerability to wider social forces. It is widely acknowledged that children are highly valued in Caribbean societies and that they are also subjected to strict regimes of discipline and punishment: 'spare the rod and spoil the child' is frequently cited as a fundamental guiding principle in child-rearing throughout the region.[6] Narratives of childhood featured prominently in early Caribbean writing and continue to do so, providing writers with a suitably porous subjectivity-in-process through which to explore questions of *becoming* that resonate with wider struggles for cultural and political autonomy.

Helen Gilbert usefully reminds us that 'childhood' is a social construction, its roots in European, post-enlightenment thought, which proposes a *developmental* narrative: with the right amount of guidance and discipline the child becomes a 'proper' adult. This rhetoric of development structured colonial attitudes: unruly natives, like unruly children, could be disciplined into conformity with European norms and mores. But, where some writers pursue a developmental line 'with its ultimate referent being the adult subject who develops – or will develop – from the child depicted',[7] Gilbert argues that Senior embeds her construction of the child-subject within debates about broader cultural questions of identity, rather than that of *individual* identity-formation.[8] In other words, Senior is less interested in tracing the child's development to adulthood in the manner of the *bildungsroman* than in exploring and exposing the socio-cultural matrix through which children, and by extension childhood, are constructed – and constrained. This line of argument is consolidated by the fact that many of Senior's stories end with the young protagonist poised on the *brink* of adulthood but seldom fully launched *into* it.

## CHILD-SHIFTING: THE CHILD AS CULTURAL CAPITAL

'The Two Grandmothers' exposes the opposing socio-cultural forces that the child-subject must navigate in the process of self-making. Through a series of monologues addressed to her mother, a child narrator chats about her visits to her two grandmothers. Grandma Del, her paternal grandmother, is black, lives in the country, keeps pigs and poultry, goes to church regularly, and tells the child stories 'not stories from a book you know, Mummy, the way you read to me, but stories straight from her head. Really!' (*ASW*: 64). 'Towser', as Grandma Elaine, her maternal grandmother, prefers to be called, is light-skinned (her servant tellingly describes her as '*almost* a fair lady' (*ASW*: 67, my emphasis)) lives in town, has boyfriends, goes to the gym, swears, smokes and drinks and indulges the child with gifts and promises of shopping trips to Miami. Although initially enchanted by Grandma Del's stories and simple, relaxed life style, as the years pass, the child succumbs to the material attractions of Towser's world (fashionable clothes, cosmetics and other American consumer goods). The story ends with the child reluctantly agreeing to visit Grandma Del on the proviso that it is a quick visit and 'We can leave there right after lunch so we will be back home in time to watch *Dallas*. Eh, Mom?' (*ASW*: 75).

The child's 'choice' has been anticipated by a series of complaints about Grandma' Del's world: no colour TV, the house is dark and crowded and her grandmother has old-fashioned attitudes to make-up. But it is the child's growing sense of her 'mixed' racial identity that forces her choice more decisively. Both grandmothers are culpable here; Grandma Del praises the child's 'honey' skin and tells her she is 'a fine brown lady' (*ASW*: 64) while Towser worries about her 'tough' hair, having already warned the child's mother that marrying a black man was a risky business, 'Honey, love's alright but what about the children's hair?'(*ASW*: 66). The child's 'fair-skinned' cousins confront the issue directly: 'You're only a goddam nigger you don't know any better. Auntie Evie married a big black man and you're his child and you're not fit to play with' (*ASW*: 73).

The child, deeply disturbed and plagued by stomach pains (whether the onset of menstruation or the physical manifestation of psychic pain is not made explicit), asks anxiously, 'Mummy, am I really a nigger?' (*ASW*: 73). What is made clear by the end of the story is that she has capitulated to the pressure to consolidate those culturally acceptable aspects of her physiognomy to which a certain status and privilege accrue.

The story presents a starkly polarized Jamaica where indigenous black Creole culture is rejected in favour of consumerist white American culture. The child's rejection of her own variously described ('black', 'brown', 'honey-coloured') body is linked with her increasing identification with 'foreign' culture and a neurotic sense of self-alienation: she is *dying* (*literally* in psychic terms) to raise her colour. Hyacinth Simpson reads the child's rejection of her 'black' grandmother as symptomatic of a wider shift away from *Jamaican* culture towards 'the foreign': 'The girl's story, as told in her own words and captured in her own voice, sends a word of warning to Jamaicans at large who allow themselves to be seduced away from their own culture and their own truth to the assumption of another's.'[9] I would argue that the story generates more ambivalent undercurrents. The obvious critique of materialist 'foreign' values is matched by a less obvious critique of 'traditional Jamaican values'. Grandma Del's religious conservatism and her self-righteous pronouncements on sinful behaviour are decidedly oppressive, values exposed as hypocritical when the child finds out that her own father was born out of wedlock (preventing her grandmother from attaining the respectability *she* craves by becoming a teacher). *Both* grandmothers invest in 'whiteness' as signifier of a 'better' life though Towser appears to have the resources which, combined with her *almost* white skin, can align her more securely with 'foreign white' cultural values. The mother to whom the child chats remains a silent, shadowy presence in this story (as does the father) and does not appear to provide her daughter with the guidance and support to enable her 'self-making', suggesting that adult figures appear to be marooned within a colonial value system, where destructive racial hierarchies remain intact despite the nationalist rhetoric of cultural plurality. Within impoverished postcolonial contexts, Senior implies, *economic* advancement is predicated upon a suppression of 'black' culture, particularly for those with the least economic clout. She is careful to indicate that to read the fear of 'turning down' (that is, being associated with black culture) as 'false consciousness' would be to underestimate the limited alternative avenues available to the less well-off. In other words, the ease with which subjects can advantageously shift along the Afro-Creole/Euro-Creole continuum depends a great deal on their class position and economic realities.

'Bright Thursdays' raises similar issues but its ending tentatively suggests an alternative to this impasse. In this story a girl-child is sent to live with her well-off father's family, the father previously having only acknowledged paternity by sending the child's mother $10. Laura's mother hopes that the child's straight nose and 'almost straight hair' will allow her to be groomed for the life of ease that she briefly hoped the child's father would rescue *her* from. 'Child-shifting' is a widespread practice in the Caribbean particularly, as Senior notes in *Working Miracles* (see pp.12–18), amongst the less well-off where children may be shifted for a variety of reasons: because a woman already has too many children while another has too few, to provide companionship or labour of other kinds to another household, because a child may have better opportunities in another household, or simply because another woman likes a particular child and the child's mother is willing to relinquish her/him.

Attempting to 'raise her colour', the child's mother rubs

Laura's skin with cocoa butter 'to keep it soft and make it "clear"' (*SL*: 39), insists she wears a hat to protect her skin from the sun and does not allow her to do the usual outdoor chores of minding goats, chopping wood or fetching water. Effectively 'withdrawn' from her community, the mother hopes that Miss Christie, Mr Bertram's mother, will be able to complete Laura's re-making. Unsure at first, Miss Christie finally capitulates, intrigued by the potential for improvement she sees in the photograph of the child sent by her mother:

> It was a posed, stilted photograph in a style that went out of fashion thirty years before. [...] Her hair was done in perfect drop curls, with a part to the side and two front curls caught up in a large white bow. In the photograph she stood quite straight with her feet together and her right hand stiffly bent to touch an artificial rose in a vase on a rattan table beside her. She did not smile. (*SL*: 42)

Here, the photograph captures the centrality of *visible*, embodied difference in the process of 'raising colour' and foregrounds the discipline required to police the girl's body into the 'right' (white) ideal: the carefully coiffed hair, the stiffly mannered pose. Once in the Bertram household, Laura notes that however poised she appears in this photo, it doesn't pass her grandmother's scrutiny: it does *not* appear with the other family portraits she examines each week as she dusts. At the Bertram household Laura is taught table manners, the benefits of a full bath each day, how to speak correctly and drop her 'country accent' and is fitted out with 'decent clothes'. Miss Christie, in other words, has the economic *and* cultural capital to consolidate Miss Myrtle's preliminary investment in 'raising' Laura's colour: 'In the child Miss Christie saw a lump of clay which held every promise of being moulded into something satisfactory'. (*SL*: 44) The village community as a whole also appears to have an investment in Laura's social 'upliftment' for when the mother is finally emboldened to approach the Bertrams for help, we are told she was 'aided and abetted by the entire village it seemed' (*SL*: 39–40). As Gilbert argues: 'Many of Senior's stories also suggest the ways in which children function as community capital in a narrative of futurity and modernisation in which the abstract idea of a child's potentiality, consistently framed as normative (Castenada 4),

30

constitutes his/her premium value.'[10] The child's mother spells out the investment in her future that being sent to the Bertram signifies:

'Laura, this is a new life for you. This is opportunity. Now don't le yu mama down. *Chile, swallow yu tongue before yu talk lest yu say the wrong thing* and don't mek yu eye big for everything yu see. Don't give Miss Christie no cause for complain and most of all, let them know you have broughtuptcy.' (*SL*: 36, my emphasis)

Laura adheres to her mother's warning, but reflects that her mother has taken her 'out of one life without guaranteeing her placement in the next' (*SL*: 46); being between cultures here implies a solitary, melancholic limbo-like existence. But Laura's unobtrusive presence in the house (she is 'seen but not heard') allows her to soak up the daily events in the adult world: 'Long before they told the child the news of her father's coming, she knew, for without deliberately listening to their conversations, she seemed to absorb and intuitively understand everything that happened in the house.' (*SL*: 50) The child engages actively in the struggle to interpret these adult machinations so that when she overhears her father dismissively telling his mother to 'stop fussing so much about the bloody little bastard' (*SL*: 53), she is able to survive this cruelty and affirm her sense of self: she runs to school and 'by the time she got to the school gates she had made herself an orphan' (*SL*: 53). Both formal education and the informal education that removal from family and community allows (or *forces*), provide the child with liberating possibilities, though the story ends before we see the achievement of this liberation. This denouement implies that formal education – despite its European provenance – can be used discerningly to provide the child with a way of making choices about cultural values that may well not align with those that her move 'up' to her aunt's house signals.

The stories discussed so far depict 'the family' as a fairly loose structure that is constantly being edited and adjusted to include or exclude individuals depending on their cultural clout (or lack of it). Rather than the tight symmetry of the nuclear family, the families presented here are porous and hybrid, not defined strictly by 'blood' relations. Bodies, too, are presented as hybrid entities whose 'natural' characteristics can (*sometimes*) be disciplined into more culturally acceptable forms. But Senior presents this hybridity as a cause for anxiety rather than celebration in a context where certain components of this 'mix' are the privileged markers of economic success. In the last two stories discussed in this chapter, 'Discerner of Hearts' and 'Ballad', creolization and hybridity *do* present more creative possibilities, ones in which children are crucial agents in recognizing and pursuing these possibilities.

### 'THINK IS ONLY BOOK HAVE LEARNING?' (*DH*: 5)

'Discerner of Hearts' gives more considered treatment to the intersection of the oral and the scribal implied in the discussion above, generating more understated registers of Creole performativity and (again) questioning, if not overturning, the socially prescribed hierarchy which values the scribal over the oral. The family in this story is relatively securely middle class and recognizably nuclear in structure: Mr Randolph is a lawyer while 'Mama' devotes her energy to grooming their three girls into polite ladyhood. Anxious to maintain their middle-class status, the parents distance themselves from the 'superstitions' of Jamaican folk culture and embrace the values of rationality and modernity. Theresa, the second of their three daughters, feels clumsy and awkward and, fearing she is the least favoured of the family, secretes herself quietly in various hiding places, an outsider of sorts, until she is 'forcibly dragged her into the family circle' (*DH*: 13). The person Theresa feels most at ease with is the feisty servant, Cissy. Despite her employers' disapproval, Cissy freely expresses warnings to the three girls about the dangers of 'Blackartman', the obeah man who snatches children to cut out their hearts to 'use', and proclaims the powers of Father Burnham, the balmyard healer who 'reads' people and heals their diverse afflictions and troubles with various herbal remedies.[11] Mr Burnham purchases milk from the Randolph family, and each time he comes Mr Randolph playfully threatens to report him to the law for his illegal balmyard practices. Cissy, who understands the children's playful mocking of Mr Randolph's mannerisms as a continuation of their father's disrespectful middle-class snobbery, tells the girls: 'Hm. You can gwan run joke. Think Father is man to run joke bout? Father is serious man. But you just like yu father. Have no respect for people. Unless their skin turn and they live in big house and they drive up in big car. But one day, one day *the world going spin the other way* though. And then we will see.' (*DH*: 7, my emphasis)

Cissy herself invokes Father Burnham's help to tempt the man she desires away from his current lover but when she succeeds and becomes pregnant, is plagued by anxieties. She fears that the abandoned woman has worked a 'bad obeah' on her and that she has misused Father Burnham's treatment by using it for 'badminded' purposes. She becomes so ill and withdrawn that Theresa, despite fearing what might lie in Mr Burnham's be-flagged balmyard, plucks up the courage to visit him. He listens attentively and Theresa is boosted by his kind words, 'You are going to grow up to be a fine lady, for you have a big, big heart. But you must stop feeling bad bout yuself' (*DH*: 25). Although Father Burnham's advice is more in the spirit of 'talking' therapies (such as counselling) and does not involve any special herbs or baths or potions, Theresa returns home and finds that she is able to 'invent' a series of treatments which she reports to Cissy as being Father Burnham's utterances. In fact, Theresa has (unwittingly?) learned these herbal remedies by heart from hearing Cissy recite them so often. So successful is this act of ventriloquism that Cissy is persuaded that she can retrieve the situation by having Father Burnham prepare a Table for her and a special bath. In the process, Theresa develops more confidence about her place in the family (and the wider world) and Cissy has cause to reflect on and re-embrace her mother's advice about respecting ancestral spirits, taking protective baths, wearing charms and 'living right'.

## 'BUT ONE DAY, ONE DAY THE WORLD GOING SPIN THE OTHER WAY THOUGH. AND THEN WE WILL SEE' (*DH*: 7)

Senior uses the intersecting stories of Cissy and Theresa to dramatize the possibilities for dialogue across differences of class, race and culture. The story constructs the child (literally and symbolically) as a go-between, able – and willing – to mediate between tightly circumscribed spheres of distinct cultural values. We learn that Father Burnham cannot read and, like many in the community, he relies on Mr Randoph 'for help with filling out forms or writing letters to the government or reading letters from the government, which were the only kinds of letters most people received.' (*DH*: 4) This places 'Justice Randolph' (as Father Burnham refers to him) in a position of considerable authority. Cissy, too, is illiterate; when teased for holding a book upside-down and 'reading', she is furious:

> 'Eh. Just because my skin black, people think I am idiot, eh? People think I fool. Just because I couldn't get to go to school like *some* backra people children, because I had was to stay home and help *my* mother look after the baby them. [...] Think is only book have learning? Ai. I wouldn't bother to tell *some* people all the things I know that they will never know. And you know why?' she would ask, suddenly eyeing each of them in turn as they cowered, ashamed, before her. [...] 'Because,' she would end triumphantly, 'no book make yet that could write down everything. Learn that!'
> (*DH*: 4–5)

Cissy articulately vocalizes her recognition of the power associated with literacy as well as the injustice of her exclusion from it. At the same time, she also vividly demonstrates her considerable vocal skills in *rebutting* the power of the printed word, terrifying the children with her performative Creole oral skills. This doesn't 'cancel out' the children's class-privileged literacy (or make the world 'spin the other way') but her words do have impact and their cowed response to her anger also implies that they sense intuitively the *righteousness* of Cissy's rage. As Senior argues, 'To create something from nothing is the art of the poor, and to have a mouth full of words is to be endowed with riches.' (*ORW*: 40)

This sense of there being alternative ways of seeing and knowing or *reading* the world is extended when explicit parallels are drawn between what specific words might mean. When asked about Father Burnham's work as a healer, Cissy suggests a world view in which words have *parallel* meanings: 'There is sick, and then again there is sick'; 'There is doctor and there is doctor.' (*DH*: 3–4) This alternative system of signification operates alongside the conventional one, resonating with its own cultural authority as when Cissy glosses the word 'reading': '"Father Burnham a great healer. A famous man. Father have the *key*. People come from all over the world to beg Father to *read* them," Cissy would boast.' (*DH*: 4) Cissy states these as matters of *fact*. Theresa has to work it out on her own terms, eventually coming to an understanding after her conversation with Father Burnham that this different definition of *reading* involves an ability to interpret the variety of signs and signals of human interaction; he really is a *discerner of hearts*. Father Burnham's practice, as Theresa understands (or translates) it, might well be described as an hermeneutics of body language, speech and behaviour that resonates with both psychoanalytic interpretation and literary readings (both of which are themselves, of course, intertwined discourses). In a lecture entitled, 'The Poem as Gardening, the Story as Su-Su', Senior elaborates on this understanding of 'reading' in Jamaican folk culture in ways that associate it with 'divining': '"Reading" is also part of the co-optation of the language of books and its use to signify something different from the perusal of words. The true "reader" is the se-er, the one with the power to see right through someone or something and reveal the truth.' (*ORW*: 44) When Theresa visits the Balmyard, a sign inside the main room lists all the services Father Burnham offers along with his qualifications:

> All welcome
> Father Burnham. M.H.C., G.M.M.W., D.D., K.R.G.D.
>> Bringer of Light
>> Professor of Peace.
>> Restorer of Confidence.
>> Discerner of Hearts.
> Consultation and advice.
>
> (*DH*: 22)

We are told that some of the writing is chaotic and badly spelt, 'But, as if the person didn't care, the painted letters were jauntily decorated which [sic] swirls and squiggles and dots.' (*DH*: 22) Although Senior chooses not to replicate these 'mistakes' on the page, this use of the paraphernalia associated with 'book learning' is indicative of respect for the power associated with the symbols of print. To quote Senior again: 'The book itself is valued as commodity only for the purchase of a better life for one's children who master it. It is perceived not as art but as symbol or talisman.' (*ORW*: 43) But this example also suggests a cheerful confidence in cavalierly redeploying symbols from one cultural arena in another; the creolised form which results can be read as an example of a refusal to be cowed by the supposed superiority of 'the book'.

'Discerner of Hearts' stages the dynamic interaction of the written and the oral with the child operating as a cultural translator or mediator – a 'secret agent' of creolization. It is worth noting, however, that despite the ease with which the child moves between her designated middle-class milieu and that of the servant's, not *everything* is easily translatable or readily apprehended; *something* remains 'unreadable'. As Cissy plans a 'Table' to ensure her baby's protection from evil, she reflects:

> But there were some things she didn't tell Theresa. For although Theresa was her friend and had a big heart, she knew that her kind of people wouldn't understand why someone like her could take the last farthing she had to her name, everything hidden under the floor board, and give it all to Father Burnham to pay for drummers and prepare for the feast [...] Wouldn't know *how badly she needed to be with her own people* dressed all in blue robes for cutting and clearing. (*DH*: 36, my emphasis)

Earlier in the story, Cissy acknowledges that 'people like Theresa didn't need that kind of protecting for nothing seemed to threaten them, people with their turn-skin and big house and big car.' (*DH*: 29) Cissy assesses and *rationalizes* her investment in 'superstitious' practices in relation to the material realities of her place in the world, making it less easy for the reader to be sceptical or to dismiss it as 'blind superstition' or 'false consciousness'. The explicit moral of the story, that kindness – 'a good heart' – facilitates the transcendance of difference, is underpinned by a realistic indication of the *material* realities that may limit the extent of identification across cultural spheres. Cissy *pretends* to read and Thersesa *pretends* to be a balmyard healer: Senior implies that we read these 'acts' as first steps towards identifying with 'the other' to move towards ethical engagements that might just make the world 'spin the other way' (*DH*: 7) to enable a more just (and perhaps more fully creolized?) future. The story hints at this possibility of social change with the prospect of Theresa teaching Cissy's child the ABC, 'as soon as he was old enough, *before* he went to school' (*DH:* 36, my emphasis). The not-yet-born child might be read as symbolizing the potential of a more fully synthesized hybridity, one that moves beyond 'juxtaposing' or 'crossing' of cultural spheres towards a 'truer' creolization.

## 'BALLAD': PORTRAIT OF THE (CREOLE) WRITER AS A YOUNG GIRL

'Ballad' enacts the most extended exploration of the possibilities for *writing* a Creole poetics. A concern with both the *form* and *theme* of the story-telling process is established in the opening sentence: 'Teacher ask me to write composition about The Most Unforgettable Character I Ever Meet and I write three page about Miss Rilla and Teacher tear it up and say that Miss Rilla not fit person to write composition about and right away I feel bad the same way I feel the day Miss Rilla go and die on me.' (*SL:* 100) Senior deftly establishes the stern prescriptions governing a written story (the teacher is absolutely sure that Miss Rilla is *not* a suitable subject) while indicating the power of story-telling (the narrator suggests parallels between the 'death' of her story at the teacher's hands and Miss Rilla's death). Interestingly, it is unclear whether the grammatical error in the title of the required composition, 'The Most Unforgettable Character I Ever Meet' is Lenora's or the teacher's. The young narrator goes on to tell the 'ballad' of Miss Rilla anyway, asserting that she *is* a fit subject for composition despite the scandal surrounding her (one of Miss Rilla's lovers murdered another man she was also involved with). In the process Lenora forges a hybrid narrative out of the gossip around her, from her own observations of Miss Rilla (as a kind-hearted, passionate and generous woman) and from the structure of the ballads she learns at school. As in many of the stories discussed above, the reader is addressed directly and assumed to be an involved participant, familiar with the various genealogies of relation-ships. Despite Lenora's reservation that 'this whole thing too deep and wide for a little thing like a Ballad' (*SL:* 100) she suggests that the chorus associated with the form can provide the necessary lament and involve the community of listeners directly: 'So I will just tell you the story of Miss Rilla and Poppa D, Blue Boy and me though is really about Miss Rilla. And when we get to the sad part we can have something like a chorus because they have that in all the ballad song they sing but I don't think about the chorus yet.' (SL: 100)

The story signals its collective construction in other ways too for embedded within Lenora's narrative about Miss Rilla are the stories she is told or overhears from the gossips in the village, particularly those between her stepmother MeMa and her friend, 'Big Mout Doris' on a number of issues and people. Both women have considerable oral skills and their gossip, peppered with proverbs, asides and detailed local genealogies, disseminates the received opinion about Miss Rilla against which Lenora calibrates her own interpretation of the woman. Where the two women speak with confidence about Miss Rilla's moral failings and the punishments that await her 'in the next life', Lenora offers evidence of Miss Rilla's observable behaviour in the present. The 'facts' of Miss Rilla's scandalous past are not narrated until four pages from the end of this thirty-four page story so that emphasis is placed less on 'the scandal' itself than on the community's *response* to it *as* scandal. Senior presents gossip as the conduit of unreliably prejudiced and salacious news *and* as a way of invoking the community as a chorus of voices, expressing the zeitgeist of the village in all its complexity, and with all its joys, contradictions, limitations and harsh prescriptions.

Other 'smaller' narratives about Lenora's family and Springville Village are embedded within the larger narrative, dispersing its designated focus. Lenora has been 'shifted' from her mother's family (to avoid the shame of being 'a Barstard around the place' (SL: 102)) and lives with her father, stepmother and their seven children. Though kind, the stepmother is a strict disciplinarian, invoking Christian mores and reminding the child repeatedly that her dubious 'pedigree', her 'natty' hair and 'extraness' (outspokenness) means that her options in life are limited. Miss Rilla, by contrast, refuses the mores that govern village life, is philosophical about her childlessness (where the gossips say 'she no better than mule because God curse is on her' (*SL*: 113)) and she refuses to be cowed by the drama of her past history, flaunting her relationships, her flashy clothes and bedspread with great *joie de vivre*. And she is attentive and generous to Lenora, encouraging and supporting her. The child is struck by the harmony of Miss Rilla's unmarried life with Poppa D; by contrast, the conventional marriage of her father and stepmother appears violently turbulent. Lenora recalls the night her father lay siege to their home firing wildly with his shotgun as the family barricaded themselves within and MeMa prayed for deliverance:

> Holy Father look down upon your innocent little children Dulcie and Lenora your precious little lambs that don't old enough yet to bring any sin into your world and thy servant who always serve you well and pay her tithe and see how this drunken son of a bitch is about to kill all of we and please God don't let him shoot we for I am your good and faithful servant Gretta Gayle amen. (*SL*: 119)

The creolized Biblical language here provides yet another resonant example of the kind of hybridity which the story itself enacts in its negotiation between literary 'ballad' and oral story. Although the father continues shooting at the house (until drink tempts him away) the violence of this encounter is tempered by Lenora's comment that her father is an extremely good shot and their survival implies that he is clearly not aiming to kill. Similarly, MeMa's prayer is a performance directed as much to the villagers who are surely witnessing the event and to her husband, as it is to God. The event, in other words, is a highly staged one in which the main protagonists self-consciously *perform* their respective roles as rampaging patriarch and wounded victim. This staged quality offsets the violence so that it functions partially as a comic interlude – though only *partially*, for however performed or rhetorical this threat of violence is, it frames the child's world. She notes early on that MeMa is 'quick to fire me a box hot-hot' (*SL*: 102) and the father is quoted as saying 'how he going to kill off the whole lot of we for we is a millstone around his neck and a bunch of parasite and a lot of other things' (*SL*: 120).

As readers/listeners we are also invited to question the construction of Miss Rilla's life as the benign antithesis to the harsh regime of the child's home. There are moments when

39

Lenora's innocence limits her view, as when it becomes apparent that Miss Rilla really *is* 'doing it in broad daylight' (*SL*: 127) with Blue Boy while Poppa D is not around. The child's narrative in 'Ballad' does not function as 'the truth' about Miss Rilla. Instead, Senior invites the reader/listener to weigh the words of the child against what we know of her (she is bright, curious, and an 'outsider' in terms of her illegitimacy *and* her willingness to embrace difference) against the words of the villagers (what we 'hear' from them suggests a reactionary conservatism and a degree of hypocrisy).

The story ends with Lenora anxiously reviewing her options; torn between studying hard to 'turn teacher with press hair and new dress' and being someone 'that can laugh and make other people happy and be happy too':

> And I tell you sometime when MeMa go on so and Teacher there nagging and all the verb and things mix up in my head I feel I can't go through with it. I don't care if I don't turn teacher with press hair and new dress. I believe it better to be someone that can laugh and make other people laugh and be happy too. And sometime I get down on my knee and pray for the Lord to come and take me so I can see for myself where Miss Rilla gone to. (*SL*: 134)

Lenora is invested with considerable agency in 'Ballad', though the melancholy note of the conclusion complicates this. She narrates Miss Rilla's story in a manner that inscribes the prejudiced stories of the community *and* her own interrogation of these versions, to create a hybrid compositional form which *can* tell the (composite) story of 'The Most Unforgettable Character I Ever Meet'. In the process, Senior manages to both invoke 'traditional' ideas of oral tale-telling with its implicit consensus of meaning *and* to inscribe a critique of such consensual modes, a self-consciousness about narration aligned more readily with the short story as a quintessentially *modern* form. Lenora narrates in a colloquial, apparently haphazard manner, inviting the reader/listener to piece together Miss Rilla as a 'character' out of fragments of information of varied provenance. The written and the spoken resonate against each other in 'Ballad' to produce a narrative not just of the flamboyant Miss Rilla but a sketch of the girl-child as woman-to-be and as story-teller/writer-to-be.

It also affirms the short story as a 'creole composition'. Unlike some of the protagonists in Senior's stories, Lenora is able to negotiate a sense of agency from *within* the predominantly black Creole village, though this is made possible largely by her willingness to embrace the difference embodied in Miss Rilla's *outsider* status. Again, Senior complicates ideas of 'authentic' Creole culture by suggesting contestations over its meanings *within* tightly knit communities like Springville. As in 'Discerner of Hearts', the girl-child is able to navigate across supposedly distinct cultural systems to create a space for herself, a space of 'creolized agency'. The wider *social* possibilities of this 'creolized agency' are not delivered in either story; in 'Ballad', Leonora *does* deliver her creolized narrative but her future choices appear so starkly *unsynthesized* that she even considers death as a welcome release. A gap remains between the possibilities for cultural creolization in *textual* form and in the *lived* experience of creole culture. In the chapter that follows, I extend the discussion of creolized possibilities and examine ideas of embodied difference more fully, particularly in relation to questions of sexuality as it intersects with ethnicity and class.

41

# 3

## Negotiating 'Difference': Femininity, Masculinity, Ethnicity

This chapter explores a selection of stories in which constructions of femininity and masculinity are central and where sexuality and ethnicity intersect in pivotal ways in the narratives. In Chapter 2, I noted the uneven and contradictory processes of creolization in the rural communities depicted. Here I want to focus on the gendered and sexualized child's body to ask questions about the way that sexuality and ethnicity intersect at the threshold between childhood and adulthood. This is particularly fraught for girl-children but for boy-children too the transition is a troubled one. This anxious in-between state becomes even more intensely fraught where the body in question is also 'racially mixed'.

There is an extensive body of scholarship on the impact of plantation slavery in disrupting family and kinship ties so that enslaved men and women were largely treated as *de-gendered* labouring bodies. Many Caribbean women writers made the black woman's body the express focus of their work as they sought both to refuse derogatory colonial representations and to articulate what was distinctive about their lived realities. This frequently took the form of representations of the *maternal* body as one to be rescued from the ravages of history; Grace Nichols' collection of poems, *i is a long memoried woman* provides an example of this kind of recuperative project. Other writers placed the mother figure centre stage as an ambivalent figure, nurturing the girl-child but also inducting her into a subordinate position in relation to men in what we might now name a 'hetero-patriarchal' structure. Dionne Brand notes the excess of maternal imagery and expresses frustration at the lack of overtly sexualized representations of black women, though she acknowledges, 'And then again it's self-preservation. In a world where Black women's bodies are so sexualized, avoiding the body as sexual is a strategy'.[1] Brand's critique is part of her larger critique of the hetero-normative focus of Caribbean women's discourses; since the publication of her essay, there has been a modest increase in texts that challenge the orthodoxy of the heterosexual as *the* normative Caribbean subjectivity.[2] Olive Senior's texts seldom engage in an explicit way with adult sexuality/sensuality and she may therefore not be the obvious choice for a discussion of sexuality and the sexed female body. But I want to argue here that her more muted register and less direct focus on these matters provide productive critical possibilities.

In *Working Miracles*, Senior catalogues the many contra-dictions involved in Caribbean women's lives: they head many households where they are often responsible for the paid and unpaid labour necessary to upkeep the home and yet women often speak of it 'looking bad' if they acknowledge this power publicly, the implication being that it makes them 'masculine women' and emasculates men. Women's *visible* strength puts 'men-in-crisis'. This attitude clearly has some bearing on why women are still under-represented at all levels in public office in the Caribbean. A similarly contradictory attitude prevails in relation to motherhood: mothers are widely revered (because of their crucial role as heads of households) and yet women are routinely denigrated in public discourses (calypso, ragga, proverbs, many religions); motherhood is the privileged symbol of value for women and yet early pregnancy is projected as 'a fall' which scuppers the girl's chances of upward social mobility. As Senior notes, 'Despite the strictness which they observe in rearing daughters, parents are anxious that the girl should by a certain age "prove herself" by commencing child-bearing.' (WM: 75)

As noted in Chapter 1, attitudes to sex and sexuality in the Caribbean veer between a prudery shaped by colonial and Christian attitudes and an energetically anti-establishment embrace of the explicitly sexual: what Cooper names, 'slackness'.

43

In *Working Miracles*, Senior also notes contradictory attitudes among the women interviewed so that recognition of sex as 'natural' was expressed alongside the need for stern vigilance as soon as a girl starts menstruating. The surveillance of girls at puberty, 'daughter-watching', was deemed necessary to ensure that girls 'made the most' of their sexuality in socially acceptable ways. Senior cites Brodber's analysis:

> But they themselves [Jamaican working class women] are convinced that sexual activity is natural and they know that in the circumstances of their lives, sex is one of their most marketable attributes and one which would facilitate their social mobility. They know that unless skilfully used, it can invalidate their goals so they continue to guard their girls against involvement in sexual activity by their militant stand against social intercourse with the opposite sex. The energy which they put into it and the failure which they see as endemic to this plan must create great frustrations. (*WM*: 72)

Fear, rather than information about sex and reproduction, is used to keep girls from 'falling' and many of Senior's stories involve girls who are disciplined for asking questions deemed inappropriately sexual. And yet, as these stories also suggest, early pregnancies are common and are, after some preliminary hostility, largely accommodated. In this contradictory and over-determined context, it is not surprising that puberty figures as a dramatically charged moment for the girl-child and that venturing into 'womanhood' is fraught and dangerous.

## CONSTRUCTING FEMININITY

If, as Senior argues, 'individuals often teeter between two or more racial and cultural ideals' (*WM*: 26) then this process is dramatized most explicitly in those stories where sexuality intensifies the anxieties of 'teetering between', a process which is the focus of 'Zig-Zag'. Laura in 'Bright Thursdays' embraces her orphan status and the possibilities provided by education; the child in 'The Two Grandmothers', terrified of the spectre of her 'nigger'-self, succumbs to the lure of consumerist, 'white' culture. Sadie, the protagonist of 'Zig-Zag', also struggles to repress those aspects of her pubescent body identified 'black' which may prevent her from achieving the dubious privileges of ladyhood. Adults again do not provide responsible guidance but instead are complicit in perpetuating paranoia about raced and sexed identity. Sadie's mother, aunt and sister all pressure her to conform to the norms of respectable femininity against the child's own preferences.

Sadie and Muffett are from a relatively impoverished but 'Good Family' (as their mother frequently reminds them) and rely on their Aunt Mim in town, to put them through high school and in so doing, upgrade their social standing. Muffet is assured a place with Aunt Mim because she has all the right physical attributes (straight hair, fair skin) *and* behaviour (she is well-mannered and ladylike). Sadie's prospects, however, are more precarious: she speaks Creole and laughs loudly ('loud and careless as a market woman' (*DH*: 158)), has tomboy ways, dark skin and wild, 'hard' hair. She also enjoys hanging about in the kitchen with Desrine, the servant whose home at the top of a steep 'zig-zag' path Sadie is eventually allowed to visit. There she befriends Desrine's eldest daughter, the beautiful 'light-skinned' Manuela who openly refers to her siblings as 'bungo pickney' and 'natty head' and whose own hair is carefully groomed with 'miracle cream' to make the most of its 'good' qualities. When Manuela accompanies Desrine to town, the three girls play an elaborate beauty-parlour game in the garden. This game comes to an abrupt end when Manuela, in her role as hairdresser, proclaims that she can't do a 'nice up-sweep' with Sadie's 'hard' hair, and that she should go to 'Madame Blackadoodoo': 'we don't do this kind of hair in this parlour [...] This kind of hair needs straightening. This is bad hair. We don't do straightening here.' (*DH*: 211) Sadie slaps Manuela across her face silencing hers and Muffet's laughter and ending the game. Instantly, each girl resumes her 'proper' place: Manuela reverts to her subservient position (as the daughter of the servant); Muffet, in line with her already established role as a mouthpiece for European/patriarchal values, hectors Sadie for 'letting this little black girl drag [her] down' (*DH*: 213). Manuela never returns and eventually Sadie learns that she is expecting a child. Muffet goes off to stay with Aunt Mim to perfect the art of becoming 'a lady', a process that Sadie, early on in the story has defined herself *against*:

45

None of them would dream of admitting they knew anything about bush and Africans, for they were busily preparing to go to high school where their fathers would pay large fees so they could be turned into ladies who would straighten their hair and rub Ponds Vanishing Cream into their faces every night and wear 4711 toilet water and learn to squeeze their bodies into corsets and their feet into tiny shoes so they would have bunions for the rest of their lives. (*DH*: 161)

The story closes with Sadie's recurring dream in which Desrine's children, lead by Manuela holding her own new baby, come ceremoniously to the house to collect Desrine. Sadie is standing at the gate as they arrive but 'they all looked right through her, as if she was invisible'. When they leave, carrying boxes of Desrine's belongings, Sadie calls 'Goodbye, Desrine' but Desrine, too, looks right through her. When she tries to follow, Sadie gets bogged down in the water hyacinths and is only able to extricate herself when her mother throws her a huge comb. The comb functions here as an ambivalent symbol: as the 'key' that might unlock a better future but also one that implies being locked-up or locked-out from other possibilities. Sadie finds herself back on the road: 'Now she had lost the desire to follow Desrine. She nevertheless turned to watch her disappear down the road, *waiting for her to spin around and wave, so she could go back to Mother Dear*. But until Desrine got too small to be seen, she never looked back.' (*DH*: 218, my emphasis) Sadie appears to require Desrine's blessing (in the form of a farewell wave) to release her from her desire to align herself with Desrine's world, which is, by implication, the 'indigenous' Jamaica, the one Sadie intuitively desires to associate herself with and in which she has immersed herself as much as the dictates of her mother allow. At the start of the story Sadie is described as a 'restless spirit' and when Desrine complains about Manuela, 'As if mad-ants biting her all the time [...] Never see a chile restless so', Sadie thinks, 'I am just like Manuela' (*DH*: 155–7). The yearned-for identification with the social/racial 'other' that Sadie expresses here cannot be fulfilled. The ending of the story leaves Sadie poised on the brink of return to her 'proper' social place, suspended limbo-like, awaiting Desrine's blessing. This moment of rupture offers a less dramatic and more melancholic reprise of a scene of rupture in Jean Rhys's *Wide Sargasso Sea* where Tia, the servant's daughter, throws a stone at Antoinette, the master's daughter, drawing blood and abruptly terminating Antoinette's longed-for affiliation with Tia.[3] By filtering the (inconclusive) conclusion of the story through Sadie's dream, Senior suggests a kind of paralysis and ennui rather than the dramatically conclusive rupture of Rhys' text. This scene of rupture might also be read in relation to Adrienne Rich's notion of 'compulsory heterosexuality', illustrating the way that female homo-social affiliations must be persistently and repeatedly short-circuited in patriarchal regimes to ensure that the girl-child takes up her designated heterosexual gender role.[4] The possibilities for tomboy behaviour and for crossing class and race boundaries are all simultaneously prohibited at puberty when playful passing across social categories (of race, gender, sexuality) becomes a more serious matter.

The racially indeterminate female body in 'Zig Zag' is represented as a site of contestation which puberty intensifies. In an insightful discussion of this story, Alison Donnell recognizes the *materiality* of the body and the way that, 'in racist societies the body as assumed racial artefact remains the priority marker through which identities are delineated'.[5] In this context, Sadie and Manuela's bodies are marked by racial signifiers that require rigorous disciplining and grooming to fix them securely in the desired social category. The two girls are not 'at home' in the very bodies they inhabit, the restlessness that characterizes them indicating ontological insecurity rather than a cause for celebration. Bodies betray by making *visible* unwelcome racial origins that are seemingly *irrefutable* signs of blackness. Manuela's 'fall' into pregnancy cancels out what little cultural capital her beauty and clear skin represent; but it also becomes a spectre of the worst that could happen to Sadie if she doesn't protect *hers*. Sexuality *per se* appears here to confirm Manuela's ethnicity – her pregnancy signals a *fall, back* into *blackness*. By comparison, Sadie's *whiteness*, precarious because it is not buttressed by economic clout, appears to demand a practically *asexual* self if she is make it to 'ladyhood'. Sadie's dream implies not only being suspended between racial categories but also between childhood and adulthood. Crossing over to the *other side* – into a fully creolized future – is presented here as perilous, if not impossible because the 'choices' are so starkly polarized. The racially in-between or 'brown'/'mixed-Creole' body does not represent as Brathwaite argues (albeit in relation to a much earlier period), 'a bridge, a kind of social cement, between the two main colours of the island's structure', that is between the Euro-Creole and Afro-Creole cultural spheres,[6] but signifies a gap that can only be crossed with relative ease in the (relative) freedom of childhood.

## CONSTRUCTING MASCULINITY

Becoming a 'woman' presents girls with stark 'choices'. The passage to 'manhood', though far less often the explicit focus in Senior's stories, is equally troubled – and troubling. 'Country of the One-Eyed God' is suggestive here; it concerns a young man on the run whose aggressive masculinity is contextualized in relation to the strict Christian faith in which his grandmother raises him. The story offers a fairly comprehensive biography of the boy who becomes 'a thief, a murderer, a hired gunman, a rapist, a jailbird, a jail breaker, and now, at nineteen, a man with a price on his head' (*SL*: 16). The boy's mother migrates in search of work and leaves the child to be raised by his grandmother, a familiar pattern in the Caribbean and one represented widely in its literature where the grandmother figure is often revered. Here, the grandmother struggles to make a living and struggles hard, too, to make the boy conform to her idea of '*righteous* living', 'A beat and a beat and it never come out. A never see a child tough so. [ ... ] But he dont get no bad blood from my family I dont have to tell you'. The grandmother concludes that it is 'the times breeding them tough pickney' (*SL*: 18) but the young man is clear that abandonment by his mother and the regular 'battering' from his grandmother are to blame, not 'blood' or 'the times'. He challenges her belief in a 'one-eyed God', who is heedless of the poor, and whose teachings are used to sanction violent abuse of children and induce blind faith in a just 'hereafter'. The story ends poised on the brink of a decisive severing of 'blood ties' as the young man slowly lifts the gun. It stands as both an exposition of male violence *and* a powerful critique of the way women are complicit in perpetuating violent regimes, with Biblical doctrines invoked to support such

48

violence. The story also profoundly challenges prevailing literary representations of the grandmother as a reliable source of nurture and sustenance.

'The Boy Who Loved Ice Cream', on the other hand, focuses on a sensitive young boy whose father worries that he may not really be his child – of his *blood* – precisely because he is *sensitive*. When the boy has nightmares and seeks comfort in his mother's arms, the father asks, 'what is wrong with this pickney eh? A mampala [effeminate] man yu raise' (*SL*: 86). The father's aggressively possessive battle with the son over the mother suggests a neatly reversed oedipal struggle, with the *father* seeking to 'kill off' the son to maintain possession of the mother; a reversal that implies the precarious hold on adulthood of the man. This possessiveness about 'his woman' extends to all other men who come into contact with the boy's mother so that the father's irrational suspicions and surveillance of the mother create an atmosphere of tension which structure the boy's understanding of his world. In the end the boy does not get to taste the much-anticipated ice cream because he is abruptly yanked away by the father after seeing the mother conversing with a man. The father's aggressive assertion of control disrupts the boy's tender approach to what might be described as a quintessential childhood pleasure. Senior's exposé of masculinity here suggests anxiety and embattlement even as it is performed in a powerfully controlling register.

'Summer Lightning' offers a more extended and nuanced focus on constructions of masculinity; it is also unusual in Senior's oeuvre in alluding directly to homosexual desire. In this story, a young boy whose mother is said to have made a 'disastrous marriage' (*SL*: 5), is sent to be looked after by his relatively well-off aunt and uncle who live in a big house in the country. An old man, a friend of the family, stays at the house for a period each year because of 'his nerves' and he takes a predatory interest in the boy. The boy, never named in the story, has only a distant memory of his parents and is left to his own devices for much of the time. He carves out a safe space for himself in 'the garden room', a small bedroom isolated from the other bedrooms. The room which 'by some architectural whimsy completely unbalanced the house' (*SL*: 1) has ten shuttered windows and three doors and provides an intriguing space of solitude for the boy to indulge his imagination (to 'explore secret places inside him' (SL: 3)), play elaborate games and establish protective rituals. When the old man comes to visit, he occupies the garden room, forcing the boy to share his secret space. The boy appreciates the gifts and the disruption to the rigid order of the house that the man's arrival brings. But he also becomes fascinated by the man's strangeness: his crooked smile, his shaky hands, trembling mouth and the way he mumbles to himself. The man also has unpleasant habits, including a 'damp mouldy smell like a dirty wet dog' and he looks at the boy 'in a sly kind of way' (SL: 4).

As the boy spends more time with the old man, Bro. Justice, the cattleman and the child's friend, becomes increasingly worried. Bro. Justice, a recent convert to Rastafarianism comes to view the boy's unquestioning acceptance of his long discourses about his beliefs as evidence that he is a prospective disciple. Bro. Justice has learned to tolerate the old man's presence but, seeing the growing friendship between the man and the boy, memories of his distaste for the man resurface. He remembers the way the old man used to watch him in the early years of his visits:

> Bro. Justice felt instinctively that for one man to look at another man like that was sinful. [...] He could not escape from the gaze of this man. Even when he was fully occupied with his chores he could feel the man watching him, would turn suddenly and there the man would be. [...] He was watching *him*. And watching him the way he should be watching a woman. (SL: 7)

Although the only physical contact the old man makes is to once lightly touch Bro. Justice's face as he passes, the gesture and the man's accompanying smile, enrage Bro. Justice: 'For years afterwards whenever the image of the man came to his mind the blood would fly to his head and he would want to annihilate that smile.'(SL: 7) When Bro. Justice expresses his concerns to the boy's aunt, she is incapable of hearing his concern for the boy or his warnings about 'Sodom' and 'sin' because she is too busy lecturing Bro. Justice about his Rastafarian lifestyle and the disrespect for her status that this seems to have engendered. The story ends in the garden room with the old man advancing purposefully upon the boy with a commanding look in his eyes while the child, sensing danger, wills Bro. Justice to hear his pounding heart and come to his rescue.

An initial reading of this ending might consolidate Bro. Justice's role as symbol of an authentic, grounded, black Jamaican culture, given Rastafarianism's roots in Jamaica. By contrast, the old man, in such a reading, would represent the intrusion of something strange and alien, if not technically 'foreign' (we are never told where he actually comes *from*) that intrudes into and violates the sanctity of the home. Bro. Justice is described as utterly reliable in the boy's eyes, someone who 'could never transform into anything but what he was' (*SL*: 2) while the old man is described as sly, strange and smelly. In this reading the old man's desires and behaviour could easily earn him the labels 'homosexual' and/or 'paedophile' though neither of these words appear in the story. The fact that he comes from 'elsewhere', might easily be interpreted in line with the fairly widespread way of representing so-called 'sexual deviancy' as a phenomenon which is imported from elsewhere ('the West'), alien and irrelevant to the region.

But this reading requires a degree of qualification in light of other factors inscribed within the narrative. It is made clear that *both* men seek to exercise their power over the child in selfish and egotistical ways and both men exploit the child's suggestibility by convincing him of the talismanic power of certain ways of doing things: Bro. Justice tells the boy that 'Lightning only strike liard' and that it is 'Jah triple vision. Is like X-ray dat.'(*SL*: 1); the old man suggests that the elephant if pointed in a certain direction will bring the boy luck. Neither of the two men is attentive to the fear and uncertainty these ideas generate in the sensitive young boy's imagination. Rather, their concern is dominated by the particular designs they have on the boy's affections, whether as potential disciple *or* lover. At one point in the narrative, as Bro. Justice reflects on the relationship between the old man and the boy, he presents this territorial tussle for the boy's affection and trust *explicitly* in terms of seduction: 'Bro. Justice could have called the child and *seduced* him back from the old man but he was too proud lest the boy think he could not continue life without him.' (*SL*: 8, my emphasis) When he remembers the way the man had looked at him when *he* was a boy, the vehemence with which Bro. Justice refuses that desiring gaze and the irrational intensity of his response, 'the blood would fly to his head and he would want to annihilate that smile' (SL: 7) suggest an anxiety about his own sexuality which, although not explicitly examined, *does* resonate in the story.

Rastafarianism is now well established as a powerful, black Jamaican cultural force, whatever the (many) challenges posed to its male-centredness: in this story, Senior is careful to note that 'in those days Rastamen were a novelty' (SL: 5). When Bro. Justice is introduced to Rastafarianism by Bro. Naptali, a visiting rastaman, he is 'deeply moved by his words and his demeanour' while the other penmen treat the visitor as 'a figure of derision' (SL: 5). Although not explored in great detail, Bro. Justice's response to Bro. Naptali's arrival is significantly different from his peers. The penmen live in the all-male environment of the barracks and the fact that their response to the visiting Rastaman shifts swiftly from alarm to derision, 'They viewed him first with alarm and then as a creature wondrous and strange' (SL: 5) indicates that he does not represent any threat to the homosocial masculinity which prevails in the barracks. Alongside this response, that of the aunt is also significant. She voices her mistrust of Bro. Justice's Rastafarianism by using the word 'queer': 'He had also been the best man on the Pen before he, according to the aunt, began to turn "queer" with his beard and his matted hair and his Bible.' (SL: 5) This clearly invites a parallel to be made with the 'strange' behaviour of the old man, who, although never actually named 'queer', is described in ways which conform to the popular stereotypes of the gay man (the sly furtive gaze, predatory behaviour, limp hand and so on). This parallel between the two men might be extended to suggest that homo*social* notions of masculinity as represented in Rastafarianism provide a contrast to the homo*sexual* behaviour and identity of the old man. The boy, caught between the competing claims of the two men, and the competing definitions of masculinity that they represent, is left at the end of the story teetering involuntarily between the two. Despite, this 'cliff-hanger' ending, there is little question that the old man's approach signals a *threat* to the boy's well-being and that Bro. Justice is hailed by the boy as his saviour. Although Bro. Justice's interest in the boy is compromised by his own egotism, the 'back story' of his conversion to Rastafarianism helps to qualify this.

The old man's 'back story', by comparison, remains mysterious with the repeated references to his 'nerves' the only explanation the reader is given of the man's illness, 'The boy did not know what nerves were except that they were alive and he could feel them pulling in the room like telegraph wires.'(*SL*: 9) The vagueness and mystery which shroud the man's illness allow familiar associations to be made between his psychological state and that of his inappropriate – or 'deviant' – sexual predilections.

So, a queer reading of 'Summer Lightning' might quite rightly critique the uncontextualized 'threat' which the old man's 'homosexuality' introduces into the home, especially as there are no other stories in this or the other collections which offer alternative representations of same-sex desire. But the fact that the reader is invited to question Bro. Justice's ability to fulfil his role as 'rescuer' compromises this neat stand-off. It is also significant that the 'home' is presented as a lonely and *un*homely space for the boy and that the aunt and uncle, as surrogate parents, offer little to suggest that the heterosexual norm of family life is being endorsed as an ideal. Finally, the fact that the old man's threat is never actually *delivered* within the narrative – and the only 'evidence' we are given of his sexual behaviour is the light caress he places on Bro. Justice's cheek – might also suggest that the reader is being invited to question the familiar, alarmist and derogatory assumptions about 'homosexuality' that the story rehearses. Whether this is an explicit intention of the author or an inadvertent effect is not important. In the context of the Caribbean where, as Timothy Chin argues, 'Caribbean literary production has traditionally maintained a conspicuous silence around issues of gay and lesbian sexuality',[7] the unresolved tensions in 'Summer Lightning' provide a space in which the reasons for this silence can be explored. The story reminds us of the conflicting, ambivalent attitudes to masculinity that are crucial to discussions of Caribbean sexuality more broadly. The story's dramatic positioning of the boy in-between masculinities, which might (crudely) be characterized as 'indigenous' versus 'foreign', also suggests interesting intersections between 'creole' and 'queer' paradigms that might be usefully pursued in the future.[8] As narratives of same-sex desire in the Caribbean become more established, as they *will* despite (and *because* of) the noise surrounding its arrival, I want to argue here that less obvious narratives of same-sex desire can also be made to generate productive contributions to these 'coming out' conversations.

## CREOLIZATION: BEYOND THE EURO-CREOLE/AFRO-CREOLE BINARY?

In this final section of the chapter, I look at 'Arrival of the Snake Woman', in which Senior tests the creolization paradigm most directly. The story is narrated in the first-person by Ish, an adult African-Jamaican male, who reflects back on the impact of an Indian woman's arrival in the Afro-Jamaican village of Mount Rose. He later credits the arrival of this woman with launching him into adulthood and out of the village. 'Miss Coolie's' role as catalyst, if not alchemist, is asserted in the first sentence of the story: 'Everything about the snake-woman was magical from the start, even the way she arrived without our seeing, though we were all looking.' (*ASW*: 1) We are never given her specific reasons for wanting to leave Montego Bay or for agreeing to come to the village as 'SonSon's woman' (he 'wins' her by pulling straws with Moses).[9] Moses is excited by the Indian woman's exotic difference, her snake-like movements and clothes, 'thin little clothes-wrap, thinner than cobweb, yu can see every line of their body when they walk'(*ASW*: 3) and offers Ish a highly idiosyncratic account of Indian indentureship by way of contextualizing her difference:

> 'Imagine come from so far to tek way black man work. [...] These coolie-woman like nayga-man,' he was saying, 'for the coolie-man is the wussest man in the whole world. If they have a wife and she just say "kemps!" – he quick fe chop off her head. So plenty of the coolie-woman fraid of the coolie-man and want the nayga-man.' (*ASW*: 3)

Where the men view Miss Coolie's ethnicity as heightening her exotic appeal, the women view her with suspicion as a 'temptress' and 'witch'. These stereotypes may perhaps be historically contextualized: some plantation owners were able to pay less for Indian than for African labourers following the abolition of slavery in 1838, causing tensions between these groups; the ratio of Indian women to Indian men was approximately 1:3, a fact which generated aggressively possessive attitudes by Indian men to the extent that the plantocracy was forced to redress the gender balance amongst indentured labour. The heightened perception of Indians as 'different' in the Jamaica of the 1950s (roughly the time in which the story is set) may also be explained by their relatively small numbers: recent census figures indicate that Indians comprised 1.3% of the total Jamaican population. In Guyana and Trinidad the percentage is much higher (over 50% in the former and over 40% in the latter). As readers, we are not given direct insights into the woman's consciousness or given her 'real' name but must rely on Ish's interpretation; she is called variously, 'snakewoman', 'Miss Coolie', 'Auntie Coolie', 'Mother Coolie', 'heathen' and 'Gertrude', when christened by Parson Bedlow.

Ish recounts Miss Coolie's progress from shy, silent arrivant to her position at the end of the narrative as the 'most prosperous citizen of the district by far' (*ASW*: 43) presiding over a large household and managing a variety of successful business ventures from 'Top House', formerly owned by the plantocracy ('old time white people') and then by Parson Bedlow. The trajectory of the narrator's own life-story unfolds as he narrates his (sketchy) understanding of hers: he has avoided Parson Bedlow's ambitions to train him for a missionary vocation, has trained overseas to become a doctor and now has his own practice in town. The boy's eagerness to help the woman when she first arrives places him in the position of cultural mediator and he teaches her the ways of the village and relays information from and about Miss Coolie to the villagers. But the roles are reversed when Miss Coolie's son, Biya, becomes ill and is refused medical treatment by Parson Bedlow, because she has refused to be baptised. Unable to reconcile the unchristian ethos of the parson's Christianity, Ish becomes ill (recognizing it later as a sickness, 'entirely of the soul' (*ASW*: 32)) and decides to distance himself from the church and the ambitions the parson has encouraged in him. He reflects that he has 'overreached' himself and become 'puffed up with pride' with his 'new knowledge' and 'book learning' (*ASW*: 33) and resolves to stay in Mount Rose and be like the other men, 'plant ground [...], hunt birds and coneys and hogs in the woods, dance the shay-shay and chase women' (ASW: 32).

But the boy's decision to commit himself to the Afro-Creole life and culture of the village is overturned decisively by Miss Coolie. She has taken her son to the hospital in town, breaking the taboos against modern medicine, which the villagers fear involve white men cutting up black men's bodies. She returns with her child recovered and, now fully persuaded by modern medicine, announces her ambitions for Ish to become a doctor and Biya, a lawyer (so he can facilitate proper land ownership papers for those in the village currently deemed 'squatters'). In the spirit of further embracing modernity and progress, Miss Coolie then goes on to join Parson Bedlow's church, accepting it as the condition necessary for her children to be accepted at the school; she agrees to a Christian marriage to SonSon and abandons her saris and bindi. Her progress thereafter from higgler, to small-goods-seller, to money-lender to successful businesswoman in Top House proceeds apace. She abandons the church as soon as the government school opens in the village and, as her economic wealth grows, is able to confidently revert back to her 'Indian' clothing and habits. The rapidity with which the phase between her arrival in the village and her arrival at Top House is narrated conveys the narrator's sense of Miss Coolie's ability to shift easily across cultures in a way that he, rooted in the village, can't.

The narrative closes with a melancholy reflection from Ish who justifies his own permanent relocation away from the village as a way of ensuring that *his* children do not have to face 'the pains of adjustment' (ASW: 42) that he did. He is filled with regret and writes his memories, the narrative we are reading, to provide his children with information about 'where we are coming from' (ASW: 45). As in many of Senior's stories, the opposing pulls of distinct cultural spheres provide the narrative tension but here the more usual Afro-Creole and Euro-Creole distinction is complicated by the inclusion of 'Indian West Indian' culture. It is also complicated by the particular history that 'Mount Rose' is given for it is presented as a place where the 'old time white people' do not have the power usually accruing to whites in Jamaica. The village 'Miss Coolie' arrives in is already 'mix-up, mix-up' (ASW: 13). Set on the very edge of the isolated area of the Cockpits, the whites on this plantation are even fewer in number than elsewhere and work alongside the blacks, out of economic necessity. The white men have had sex with black women to the extent that the village is populated with 'a whole set of white-black, mulata people' (*ASW*: 13), complicating definitive racial boundaries. By the time 'Miss Coolie' arrives, the younger generation of 'whites' have already left and the only whites in the village are the American parson and his wife. The villagers distinguish between these two 'varieties' of white arrivants in a manner that implies that hard labour and limited leisure time and money blur racial differences: 'These old-time white people were more like the black people than Parson Bedlow because they were out in the sun all day and burnt black and brown and drank rum and coffee and smoked jackass rope and cussed bad words worse than the black people.' (*ASW*: 12)

Senior constructs Mount Rose as a place that is already, at least in part, racially creolized. It is also already culturally creolized in that the villagers have accommodated the spiritual leadership of Papa Dias (whose divining derives from his Oyo grandfather), Mother Miracle (who converted to the Sixty Revivalists) *and* Pastor Bedlow (whose Christianity the villagers 'convert' to, like Miss Coolie, in order to access 'book-learning' while still participating in Papa Dias and Mother Miracle's practices). In this context, Miss Coolie's Indianness is a completely 'new' cultural phenomenon to most of the villagers. Although the boy says that her 'skin was as dark as ours' (*ASW*: 5), she is more culturally foreign to them than the whites have become. At key moments, however, Miss Coolie *is* described as 'blending in'. The first of these is when she gives birth and all the women rally round, 'For a baby, after all, made all women the same' (*ASW*: 25); later she is described joining the village women in the early dawn as they head to market to sell their produce, 'in the darkness, she looked no different from the black and mulatto women of the district carrying their goods to market.' (*ASW*: 39) Ameena Gafoor reads this as evidence of 'Miss Coolie's' willingness to 'immerse herself into the creolization process',[10] something she argues the *narrator* recognizes but the *author* is more ambivalent about, demonstrated in moments of direct authorial intervention. So she reads the shift from images of Miss Coolie 'blending in' to the final image of her as matriarch and business-woman as indicative of the author falling back on stereotypes of 'the' Indian woman (perhaps similar to those evoked by V. S. Naipaul of the Tulsi women in *A House for Mr Biswas*).[11] Gafoor cites the passage where Ish reflects on Miss Coolie's arrival: 'It was as if, crossing over the mountains to start a new life, or perhaps even earlier when she crossed the seas, she had left behind all that reminded her of the old, shed her identity and her history, became transformed into whatever we would make of her, our Miss Coolie.' (*ASW*: 7) And she concludes:

> This, again, is the conclusion of an objective perception for, while to the narrator she has creolised completely, the author still has her in the image of the capitalist Indian money-lender on the hill, complete with sari. I find this problematic or perhaps this is the kind of ambivalence which characterizes perceptions of the Indo-Caribbean woman. [...] Therefore, the denouement of the work can be seen as revealing the author's anxiety over assimilation and racial integration.[12]

I agree with Gafoor that Ish's account does not acknowledge the personal cost to Miss Coolie of her acculturation, or 'the yielding involved in the process of readjustment and accommodation'.[13] Gafoor reads this gap in understanding as the *author's* anxiety about 'racial integration', an author she defines in the essay as 'a mixed Creole woman',[14] presumably implying that there is a clear gap between the author's experience and those of her fictional constructs whose racial identity she does not share.

It strikes me, however, that Senior is offering a *critique* of Ish's interpretation of Miss Coolie's success. His un-nuanced perception of Miss Coolie's integration/creolization is shaped by the way it functions to define his own success as a doctor *away* from his village roots. In other words, Ish is both narrator and main focal point of a narrative whose concern with the Indian woman is largely *instrumental*. Miss Coolie remains 'other' because she functions as a defining trope for Ish in his quest to 'elevate' himself. Senior deploys Miss Coolie as a catalyst for change, 'a floating signifier' to expose the limitations of the *narrator's* (as well as the villagers' and Parson's) view of *difference*. Unable to rise to the challenge of a creolized future for himself, Ish asks, 'how could I set up a practice in such a backward place?' (*ASW*: 42) But he remains troubled by this and guilty that although

Biya also left the village to study, he has returned to make his future there, helping the villagers to secure their rights to the land. Ish ponders: 'And sometimes I am still unsure of my own self, of who I am, of where I belong, still feeling halfway between the old world where my navel-string is buried and the new, [...] not feeling, like Miss Coolie, at ease enough to shift fully into the relentless present.' (ASW: 44–5) Ish's narcissistic concern for what he has lost by *not* staying allows him to project onto Miss Coolie a heightened mobility and freedom that he explains thus:

> She became a free agent with a flexibility that enabled her to soar above our world [...] A flexibility that enabled her to 'do business' with family, friend, or the white man [...] Miss Coolie, in short, is our embodiment of the spirit of the new age, an age in which sentiment has been replaced by pragmatism and superstition by materialism. (ASW: 44)

Contrary to Gafoor, I don't think the narrator sees Miss Coolie as having *creolized* but as having strategically negotiated a life for herself in Mount Rose in a way that he could not. In other words, it is more a comment on *his* failed creolization than it is a comment on the success of *hers*. Ish's attitudes to creolization are altogether more ambivalent than say, Gafoor's. And this perhaps gets to the crux of what is at stake in the story.

Discussion of the extent and degree of Indian commitment to creolization processes in the Caribbean, particularly in Guyana and Trinidad, has a long and fraught history. There remains a widely held perception that Indians have focused on retaining their cultural and religious identities and have not fully and freely thrown themselves into the creolized post-colonial Caribbean nations where they have made their lives for over a hundred years. Senior's *Encyclopedia of Jamaican Heritage*, includes the following comment from a 1999 publication by Mansingh and Mansingh that conveys this duality of Indo-Caribbean experiences, 'They have shown ingenuity in maintaining a distinct religious and/or cultural identity while merging their aspirations and future with the rest of their Jamaican compatriots.' (EJH: 244) Ish's attitude to Mount Rose suggests unease about the distinct *Afro*-Creole culture that has defined his childhood, 'we still floundered around in a confused

59

tangle of emotions, family ties, custom and superstition.' (*ASW*: 44) He interprets Miss Coolie's ability to manoeuvre successfully in Mount Rose as a result of her ability to embrace 'modern' ideas of progress, 'sentiment has been replaced by pragmatism and superstition by materialism.' (*ASW*: 44) Ish recognizes that *material* wealth allows Miss Coolie the flexibility to perform the cultural identity of her choice, indicated in her 'reverting to wearing saris again, ones with gold and silver borders now' (*ASW*: 43). The trajectory of Miss Coolie's life in Mount Rose is one in which the embrace of creolization is a *strategic* one. For Gafoor, creolization signifies a more integral, politically and ethically motivated commitment to Caribbean Creole cultures than this.

As I have argued in the previous chapter, many of Senior's stories suggest a tension between Afro-Creole life and culture in rural Jamaica and the pull of 'the modern', whether that is city-life in Kingston or in 'foreign'. The lure of material values and the fetishizing of consumer goods are often presented as a cause for concern and regret. The nostalgia that haunts Ish for the life left behind, the sense that he is still 'halfway between the old world where my navel-string is buried and the new' (*ASW*: 44) is one that figures as an undercurrent throughout Senior's short stories. It is a tension that remains unresolved and is perhaps unresolvable. For just as 'Arrival of the Snake Woman' concerns a narrator whose connection to the 'country' of his past has its most tangible embodiment in the narrative he writes to pass on to his children, so too Senior's stories might be read as thematizing this primal loss. In the context of discussions of creolization, what this loss also frequently signifies is lost opportunities for a fully creolized future given the impact of new forms of cultural dominance, particularly from America.

But even if we read the story as I suggest as a critique of the limitations of Ish's ability to be a 'success' while maintaining his roots in Afro-Creole culture, it is clear that the story does not provide alternative representations to familiar stereotypes of 'the' Indian women. Indeed, it could be argued that the story ends by replacing one stereotype of the Indian woman (exotic, sensuous) with another (matriarchal, materialistic). As Gafoor suggests, the story ends with Miss Coolie in the stereotyped 'image of the capitalist Indian money-lender'.[15] Miss Coolie's money-lending *is* presented as a *categorical* difference in that she charges interest, a practice which is explicitly described as 'foreign' to the villagers who are used to a system of bartering and reciprocity; 'Miss Coolie was "in business"' (*ASW*: 40). In the broader context of Caribbean women's writing where, as Roseanne Kanhai argues, 'Indo-Caribbean women remain a token presence in the predominantly Afro-Caribbean feminist discourse',[16] the 'burden of representation' is perhaps so great here that Senior's choice of focalizer becomes risky. Brinda Mehta, in her pioneering book, *Diasporic (Dis)Locations: Indo-Caribbean Women Writers Negotiate the Kala Pani*, notes at the outset the paucity of literary material available to sustain her own analysis and refers to Senior's 'Arrival of the Snake-Woman' as a story that reveals the 'thinly disguised disdain for the Indian presence in the Caribbean', drawing attention to Senior's use of the word 'coolie' as 'a racialized epithet of inferiority and alterity'.[17] There is no question that this *is* a derogatory term but Senior's use of it has to be read in relation to the commitment in her short fiction to recording the lives of 'ordinary' Jamaicans – *and* the language in which they speak. In 'Arrival of the Snake-Woman' (and many other stories), 'nayga' is a term also used frequently and it too is deployed in an equally casual and unmarked way in line with everyday parlance.

As with the anomalous representation of (potentially) queer subject matter in 'Summer Lightning', I propose a more generous reading to embrace rather than censure this risk. I'd begin by reiterating that the limited dimensions of 'Miss Coolie' as a 'character' is a problem of narrative construction: the choice of a child narrator and a narration which loosely follows the trajectory of the *bildungsroman*, cannot be stretched to meaningfully explore the Indian woman's subjectivity without compromising the main focus of the narrative – Ish's development into adulthood. This story proceeds in a realist mode, so that the writing is constrained by what is possible textually within realist conventions and by the manifest reality *outside* the textual world upon which the author draws. Perhaps too, the repertoire of literary representations of 'Indian Caribbean subjects' available for writers (like Senior) to draw upon remains insufficiently diverse. The complexity of Indian cultural life has not yet been fully woven into the fabric of Caribbean textuality.

There are, nevertheless, possibilities for enquiry suggested in the many *aporias* in Senior's text that indicate the difficulty of textually negotiating those ethnic differences which are outside of the more familiar white/black Euro versus Afro-Creole dichotomy that defines Caribbean literature and provides the main focus of Senior's oeuvre.[18] Why, for example, aren't we told Miss Coolie's reasons for leaving Montego Bay? What is the exact nature of her relationship with her Afro-Creole husband with whom she has children who are all given 'Indian names'? Might we read Biya's commitment to stay in Mount Rose where he works for the villagers and has fathered many children with 'the local girls' (*ASW*: 43) as the beginnings of a more fully creolized (or indeed, 'douglarized'?) future than the narrative can deliver on in the historical moment in which it is set? And, finally, to return to the problem of Miss Coolie's materialism, might we read this in connection with the recurring sense in Senior's stories that economic security *does* provide individuals with agency and the flexibility to choose, even if it is not as dramatically charged as in Miss Coolie's rise to Top House. In other words, the trajectory mapped in 'Arrival of the Snake-Woman' also resonates with a question posed in Senior's stories about who can *afford* to be a creolized subject and *how*. This, I would argue, is a question that frequently underpins the anxiety of being caught between cultures that Senior's stories rehearse.

Nigel Bolland argues persuasively that the Caribbean middle classes invested in the folk and in cultural creolization in order to legitimize claims to national independence and to mobilize mass support for independence. He argues:

> More specifically, the cultural and populist aspects of the creole-society viewpoint, with its emphasis upon the origins of a distinctive *common* culture as a basis for national unity, constitutes the ideology of a particular social segment, namely a middle-class intelligentsia that seeks a leading role in an integrated, newly independent society.[19]

This essay provides a useful reminder of the politics involved in championing creolization, prompting questions about what is at stake and for whom? Olive Senior's representation of the difficulty and costs of embracing Creole culture resonates well with Bolland's arguments. It is useful to note briefly here those stories in which Senior deals directly with the failure of middle-class led, nationalist politics in post-independence Jamaica and its strategic deployment of 'race' and culture. In 'The Tenantry of Birds' (*ASW*: 46–61), a young woman, groomed by an ambitious mother to escape the 'nigrish' culture of her relatives in the country (the folk songs, ring games and 'green bush' spells), marries a bright academic who becomes adviser to the Prime Minister. The story traces the parallel trajectories of the husband and wife as they become estranged in the politically charged context of post-independence Jamaica. As he moves up the political ladder, he requires his wife to become more entrenched in conventional roles of wife and mother (eventually dispatching his family to Miami for their safety) while he acquires a radical, black PA/mistress who wears an Afro, swears, drinks and is loudly argumentative. In contrast to the wife's considered re-investment in black 'bush' culture, the husband's alignment with black cultural politics is exposed as entirely opportunistic and misogynist. In 'The Glass-Bottom Boat' (*DH*: 106–34), changing gender roles in post-independence Jamaica are presented from the perspective of a husband who, unable to keep pace with the changing cultural and racial politics of postcolonial Jamaica, finds himself abandoned in the marital home as his wife becomes increasingly 'liberated'. The husband, although sympathetically presented, is unable to interpret the changes in his wife's behaviour, misreading his wife's decision to cut off her long hair and 'go Afro', for example, as a direct assault on *him* (he sees her hair, in effect, as his property). Unable to understand her negotiation of her changing role and place in a rapidly changing 'modern' Jamaica, he appears not to be able to muster the cultural resources necessary to accom-modate to a rapidly creolizing milieu.

Finally, in 'The View From the Terrace' (*ASW*: 90–111), Senior explores the changing political and cultural landscape of post-independence Jamaica from the point of view of a 'brown' Jamaican man who, now retired, becomes obsessed by the arrival of a black woman (and her ever-expanding family) whose house blocks 'his' view over the valley. Mr Barton has devoted his life to mimicking white culture and must now adjust to these new times when: 'anything was possible, even the old beliefs and superstitions which had lasted hundreds of

63

years were being swept away, everyone now believed he was a god, tossed aside was all habit, all rules, all certainty.' (*ASW*: 91) That he bemoans the loss of 'old beliefs and superstitions' is less an indication of his investment in the power of those Afro-Creole cultural forms (as was the case, say, for the protagonist in 'The Tenantry of Birds') than an indication of his view of 'the past' as something ordered and unchanging. Barton, although presented with some sympathy, is both out of place *and* out of time. Senior quickly sketches in the way a reversal of the colonial racial hierarchy has generated new stereotypes: Barton muses that he has never, unlike many of his contemporaries, 'had a real black woman' (*ASW*: 102) and when he draws parallels between the woman in the 'shack' below and paintings of black women he has seen in Madrid, he becomes fearful of being crushed by her/their elemental power. When he remarries, Barton is at first mesmerized by Josie's white 'almost translucent' skin but discovers that she 'was incredibly vulgar, the kind of woman who no longer knew her place, like the facety little black girls nowadays' (*ASW*: 105). Barton romanticizes the black woman on 'his' hill as elemental and naturally womanly, unlike the modern, brash, women who mix-up cultural codes and refuse to perform their racially designated roles. Barton's stumbling journey towards an appreciation of the black woman might, by extension, be read as a (very) belated and (very) partial embrace of creolization. When he discovers that his faithful servant, Marcus, is the father of some of the woman's children, the small sympathetic insights that Barton has toiled towards in his reflections from the terrace are shattered: 'The woman was no better than the rest of them! A common whore!' His outrage about the woman is compounded by the fact that knowledge about 'his' servant has also eluded him, 'It was unthinkable! And he had known nothing. Nothing. How monstrous to live with someone for so many years and not know them, not know them at all!' (*ASW*: 111) A similar resistance to changing racial horizons is evident in 'Window' where an impoverished white employer, abandoned by her husband, lives with her daughter in their ramshackle family home, together with her servant. The intimate relationship between 'Madam' and 'Maid' is described by the former's daughter, Brid as being, 'intertwined like the scotch-man fig which grew on to the big silk-cotton tree, twisting and embedding itself into the trunk of the other to such an extent that it was hard to figure out which was the silk-cotton and which the fig' (*DH*: 63). Despite this close entanglement, when the servant's son suggests he might marry Brid with whom he has fallen in love, his mother declares he must be 'mad' and argues, 'you know oil and water don't mix from morning' (*DH*: 67). The servant's son is now well-off and prepared to marry Brid and buy and renovate the ramshackle 'great' house for them all to live in but this dramatic change in economic fortunes and the shift in class positions it implies is not enough to overturn a deep-seated racial hierarchy.

These stories suggest that post-independence cultural politics has clearly not delivered the 'out of many, one' motto of the new nation; it may have unsettled and even reversed a colonialist racial hierarchy but it has not generated the dynamic synthesis of cultural differences suggested in the creole-society model that was such a strong factor in promoting nationalism. Where *child* narrators seem able to respond to racial distinctions with bafflement as well as open-minded generosity, adult narrators tend towards crude judgements and are limited by their entrenched anxiety about upward social mobility. As a result they seem doomed to miss the opportunities that creolization signals.

Senior's focus in the short stories on the diverse ways that Jamaican subjects negotiate their lives in the context of the racially and culturally complicated pre- and postcolonial realities of Jamaica, offers a range of perspectives on the unevenness of creolization. If the stories thematize the zig-zagging between cultural worlds required of many Jamaicans, the reader too is required to navigate across the diverse range of stylistic contours that she deploys. Although largely realist in style, Senior draws on story-telling traditions of varied prove-nance, invoking traditional oral forms as well as those associated with more self-consciously literary narrative forms. Whether it is the cliff-hanger endings of 'Summer Lightning' and 'Country of the One Eye God'; the circuitous immediacy of 'Ballad'; the embedded narratives in 'Lily, Lily'; the conversa-tional tone of 'The Lizardy Man and His Lady'; the agonized voice print of 'You Think I Mad, Miss' or the many stories that end with protagonists poised on the brink of uncertain futures, Senior's stories tend to eschew any didactic authorial opinion in favour of an open-endedness that requires the reader to tease out possible meanings. In many ways, the reader is invited to align herself with the many protagonists in Senior's short fiction positioned in interstitial spaces, on the edge of, outside, or in between cultural worlds who must, of necessity, learn to listen, eavesdrop and overhear so that, like Anansi, they 'ketch wise'. Like Brid in 'Window', who prefers to remain unseen, the reader of Senior's short fiction oeuvre becomes adept at, 'seeing through cracks in walls and half-pulled shutters, from behind closed doors and between floorboards' (*DH*: 57). In the following chapter, I discuss Senior's poetry and argue that here too the reader is invited to read Anansi-wise, to spin meanings out of the polished fragments that characterize her poetics.

# 4

# Nature Studies: Olive Senior's 'Down-to-Earth' Eco-Poetics

landscape is its own monument: its meaning can only be
traced on the underside. It is all history[1]

The titles of Olive Senior's four collections of poetry all signal an
explicit focus on the natural world: *Talking of Trees, Gardening in
the Tropics, Over the Roofs of the World* and *Shell*. This chapter
explores how 'nature' functions in the poems, whether it is the
'nurturing green' of Senior's childhood environment in Cockpit
Country or her broader concern with the impact of colonial
history on shaping the contours of Caribbean landscapes and
the perception and representation of those landscapes. Senior
documents the flora and fauna of Jamaica, wryly observing
parallels between humans and their natural environment and
worrying away at the troubled meanings of 'nature' in the New
World. But what does – and *can* – 'nature' mean in the context of
the Caribbean where the devastation of human and ecological
resources has been so dramatic? And where far-reaching
colonial interventions have transformed the natural environment making it difficult to pinpoint precisely what is 'native' to
the region in the first place? In Senior's poem, 'Colonial Girls
School', the speaker outlines the systematic way that the
realities of Caribbean geography were denied while those of
'elsewhere' were inscribed deeply into memory:

Studying: *History of Ancient and Modern*
Kings and Queens of England
Steppes of Russia
Wheatfields of Canada

There was nothing of our landscape there
Nothing about us at all

(*TT*: 26)

DeLoughrey et al in their introduction to *Caribbean Literature and the Environment*, state the broader case clearly: 'there is probably no other region in the world that has been so radically altered in terms of human and botanic migration, transplantation, and settlement as the Caribbean.'[2] In the context of far-reaching colonial disruptions of the natural environment, geography and history become inextricably linked, making attachment to one's immediate place of birth a complicated, self-conscious and often ambivalent process.

Lloyd Brown, in the first major study of West Indian poetry, argues that 'the nineteenth century is the heyday of a Caribbean pastoral in which hackneyed nature verse in the Romantic mode alternates with the colonial's embarrassingly sycophantic verses in praise of the British Empire'.[3] He argues that a shift away from this 'derivative pastoral' required an aesthetic grounded in the region's distinctive natural environment. Many critics and writers shared this view. Derek Walcott, for example, drew attention to the colonial presumption that the Caribbean's tropical climate precluded the very possibility of art: 'But our contemners who see this climate as seasonless and without subtlety also see us as a race without temperament, therefore without any possibility of art. [. . .] *How dumb our nature is then.*'[4] While Kamau Brathwaite, in his seminal essay, 'History of the Voice', argued: 'the hurricane does not roar in pentameter'.[5] And in *The Middle Passage* V. S. Naipaul suggests that he was unable to really *see* the landscape he grew up in until his return to Trinidad as an adult – and a writer: 'Everyone has to learn to see the West Indies tropics for himself. The landscape has never been recorded'.[6] Helen Tiffin summarizes this trajectory neatly: 'For Caribbean writers, representation of the Caribbean land-scapes is thus particularly complicated, imbricated as it is in crucial ways with histories of transplantation, slavery, and colonialism and with imported European traditions of land and landscape perception and representation.'[7] By 1985, when Senior's *Talking of Trees* was published, Walcott, Brathwaite, Naipaul and many others had begun the process of recording Caribbean land and seascapes. By this time, too, widespread disappointment with the fruits of political independence had complicated representations of place further as partisan politics made celebratory acknowledgements of 'homeland' much less easily sustained.

Senior's engagement with and representation of the natural world offers a range of insights into these concerns. 'Homescape', the first poem in her first collection of poems, *Talking of Trees*, opens with an affirmation of a knowledge-base rooted in the Cockpits environment of Senior's childhood home and laments the intrusion of the modern:

> I was born with the knowledge
> of mountains and solitaires
> till jet planes and sky scrapers
> seduced this to
>
> mountains alone and one note
> of the solitaire

> (*TT*: 1)

In interviews Senior often remarks on the profound impact of the distinctive landscape of Cockpit Country on her life and writing; it is worth pausing here briefly to note its characteristics. Located inland some 130 miles north-west of Kingston, Cockpit Country is rugged terrain comprised of yellow and white limestone karst. The 'Cockpits' straddle five of Jamaica's parishes and is made up of some 5,000 hillocks with rounded peaks, steep sides and bowl-shaped depressions at their base. These formations drain water through porous bedrock and sinkholes connected to a complex, subterranean network of caves. The area, which derived its name from the 17th-century British occupiers because of its resemblance to the cock fighting arenas prevalent in Britain at the time, is fairly inaccessible and cut off. This inaccessibility proved crucial to the runaway slaves who formed a substantial Maroon community in the Cockpits when they fled from the plantations. In 1738, the Cockpit Country Maroons managed to pressure the British to sign a treaty with them recognizing the rights of the community to live there without interference from the British. Many descendants of this maroon community continue to live in Cockpit Country today. The area now provides a home for many species native to Jamaica which have become endangered elsewhere in the country. Its appeal to researchers and conservationists means it is promoted as a location for ecotourism, rather than the hedonistic tourism with which Jamaica is more frequently associated.[8]

In some poems this landscape is remembered and treasured as a space of tranquillity, as in 'Cockpit Country Dreams':

> In Cockpit Country
> the hours form slowly like stalagmites
> a bird sings
> pure note
> I-hold-my-breath
> the world turns and
> turns
>
> .    .    .    .    .    .
>
> green nurtured me

(TT: 3)

Here, the speaker's lived landscape is aligned with a temporality and sense of space which is emphatically *not* that of the jet plane or skyscraper. Instead, Cockpit Country is represented as a space of enclosure and isolation, beyond the demands of modernity, where the poet can attend in microscopic detail to the natural world and learn to decipher – or 'read' – its secrets: a literary laboratory, if you will. In 'Snail', for example the speaker warns that in ignoring the silvery trail of a snail, 'so slow/ so low', we risk missing 'what might be/ the cosmic/ trail.' (GT: 70) In each of the four collections of poetry there are several poems in which Jamaican flora and fauna are 'read' in ways that demonstrate intimate knowledge of these forms as well as wry musings on what humans might learn from them. Indeed, Senior's work in documenting some of Jamaica's plant and animal species provides an interesting supplement to her more straightforwardly archival writing (discussed in detail in Chapter 6).

Alongside the poems in which nature is observed, 'read' and memorialized, are poems which expose the long history of exploitation of natural resources in the Caribbean – plant, animal *and* human. 'Meditation on Yellow' uses 'yellow' as the organizing motif to explore the 'five hundred years of servitude' (GT: 16) following on from Columbus' 'discovery' of the islands. The speaker lightly puns on the title of Marquez's novel, *One*

70

*Hundred Years of Solitude* and his observation of 'The yellow of the Caribbean seen from Jamaica at three in the afternoon' provides both epigraph and pretext. The history of exploitation of natural and human resources in the New World is narrated by a representative Caribbean speaker signalled by the frequent shifts between 'I' and 'we' and the different identities these pronouns suggest. In the early part of the poem, the speaker identifies with 'the Indians': 'We were The Good Indians/ The Red Indians/ The Dead Indians' (*GT*: 13) while later in the poem a black/African identity is implied:

> At some hotel
> overlooking the sea
> you can take tea
> at three in the afternoon
> served by me
> skin burnt black as toast
> (for which management apologizes)
>
> (*GT*: 14)

The first section of the poem sketches in the history of barter, robbery and violence of the first encounter between the native people and the Spanish:

> so in exchange for a string of islands
> and two continents
>
> you gave us a string of beads
> and some hawk's bells
>
> which was fine by me personally
> for I have never wanted to possess things
> I prefer copper anyway
>
> (*GT*: 11)

The obsessive desire of the Spanish for gold is placed in stark contrast to the modest and understated desires of the Amerindian speaker. The poem then switches to contemporary Jamaica and to a speaker whose 'skin [is] burnt black as toast/ (for which management apologizes)' (*GT*: 14). Here tourism is presented as the 'new' narrative of discovery and conquest, continuing the history of exploitation and commodification. The speaker catalogues the services and labour that have had to be delivered (in a series of 'doing verbs': cane-cutting, loading

71

bananas, peeling ginger, chopping cocoa, mining aluminium and so on) before deciding that the relentless demands of the present-day tourist are the final straw:

> But still they want more
> want it strong
> want it long
> want it black
> want it green
> want it dread
>
> Though I not quarrelsome
> I have to say: look
> I tired now
>
> (GT: 14)

After listing all the natural resources, in addition to labour, that have already been demanded, delivered and taken (gold, land, breeze, beaches, sand, sugar crystals) the speaker concludes:

> And I reach to the stage where
> (though I not impolite)
> I have to say: lump it
> or leave it
> I can't give anymore
>
> (GT: 16)

The poem catalogues the relentless commodification and consumption of natural and human resources, concluding with the contemporary construction of the Caribbean as a place where the tourist, weary from a fast-paced Western lifestyle, can 'get away from it all' and discover paradise for her/himself. Mimi Sheller's discussion of what she calls, 'the binding mobilities of consumption' is relevant here:

> The Caribbean has been repeatedly imagined and narrated as a tropical paradise in which the land, plants, resources, bodies and cultures of its inhabitants are open to be invaded, occupied, bought, moved, used, viewed, and consumed in various ways. It is represented as a perpetual Garden of Eden in which visitors can indulge all their desires and find a haven for relaxation, rejuvenation, and sensuous abandon.[9]

'Meditation on Yellow' draws attention to this history of consumption but also asserts the right of 'the native' to consume: the poem ends with the speaker asserting her right to *leisure* and indulgence (sitting on the verandah 'overlooking the Caribbean Sea/ drinking real tea/ with honey and lemon' (*GT*: 16). Senior deftly manoeuvres her way through centuries of oppressive history before offering an image of the labourer enjoying a longed-for reversal of roles as consumer:

> making me feel mellow
> so mellow
>
> in that Caribbean yellow
> at three o'clock
>
> any day now.

(*GT*: 18)

'Any day now' resonates with both the deferred fulfilment of desire *and* with a threatening prophecy that justice *will* prevail. The tone of voice in which the speaker's anger is articulated is double-edged and dissembling, combining a respectable tone (as in the equivocating asides, 'Though I not quarrelsome', 'though I not impolite') with a more threatening register, 'Had I known [that the conquistadors were coming] I would have/ brewed you up some yellow fever-grass/ and arsenic' (*GT*: 11–16). In a powerful polemic against tourism, Jamaica Kincaid argues:

> Every native would like to find a way out, every native would like a rest, every native would like a tour. But some natives – most natives in the world – cannot go anywhere. They are too poor. [...] so when the natives see you, the tourist, they envy you, they envy your ability to leave your own banality and boredom, they envy your ability to turn their own banality and boredom into a source of pleasure for yourself.[10]

'Meditation on Yellow' insists on representing this yearned-for reversal of roles of 'native' and 'tourist' though with less of the scathing anger that characterizes Kincaid's essay. The poem is delivered in a voice that shifts seamlessly and economically between Jamaican Creole and Standard English registers, and between the declamatory and the more reflective. In both of the examples cited above ('Though I not quarrelsome', 'though I not impolite'), the omission of 'am' quickly registers that it is a Creole-speaker without necessarily implying a *full* performance

73

of that Creole identity. This establishes a Creole register which appears less concerned with naturalistic representation of Creole than with establishing a concerned and credible position from which to speak across centuries from within oppressive realities. That the speaker of this poem is presented as representative of Caribbean peoples across distinct ethnicities (and temporalities) also contributes to the sense that a more *truly* hybrid voice is being sought, expanding the parameters of Creole beyond the familiar Jamaican Creole *versus* Standard English. Further, in seeking to speak from within a continuum which includes an (imagined) Amerindian imaginary, Senior extends the repertoire of representations which has tended to portray Amerindian culture from outside of the parameters of contemporary cultural concerns within the Caribbean.[11]

In 'Rejected Text for a Tourist Brochure', Senior returns to the idea of the 'island paradise' exhausted of its flora and fauna: coral, sand, birds, turtles and iguanas. Ruthless land developers, local investors and greedy tourists all contribute to the steady erosion of resources and the speaker, with heavy irony, invites the reader to come for 'the Final Closing Down Sale' before concluding:

> Oh, them gone already? No Problem, Mon.
> Come. Look the film here.
> Reggae soundtrack and all. Come see
> my land. Come see my land and know, A-oh,
> that she was fair.

(ORW: 54)

The title, 'Rejected text for a Tourist Brochure' and epigraph ('*I saw my land in the morning/ and O but she was fair*' from M. G. Smith's poem, 'Jamaica') provide important points of reference. The title declares its ironic approach while the poem itself inscribes precisely the *not-said* of the tourist brochure: the devastation of the very same natural resources which supposedly attract the tourist and investor in the first place. But the poem is also positioned interestingly between two moments of cultural history and, to some extent, two conventions for representation. M. G. Smith's well-known and frequently anthologized 'Jamaica', first published in 1938, represents an earlier, more reflective and optimistic moment in Caribbean literary history when assertions of belonging and celebrations of landscape were more hopeful and proud. The opening stanza of Smith's poem conveys this:

> I saw my land in the morning
> And oh, but she was fair,
> The hills flamed upwards scorning
> Death and failure here.[12]

The concluding stanza of Senior's poem, by contrast, delivered in the frenzied tone of a tour operator whose exclusive motivation is profit, highlights the easy shift from selling 'the last of...' to selling 'the end' or ruination of the island itself: a film complete with 'Reggae soundtrack and all'. Here, reggae is devoid of the 'consciousness raising' qualities originally associated with it and has become the banal soundtrack to a spurious fiction of a laid-back Caribbean lifestyle. Senior replays Smith's 'And oh, but she was fair' and modifies it with small but crucial changes: '...Come see my land and know, A-oh/ that she was fair' (*ORW*: 53–4). The Creole speaking voice here is that of the stereotypically 'laid back native' with the 'Ah-oh' encapsulating a flippant refusal to see the tragedy of the situation. The poem provides a scathing critique of the degradation of both the natural *and* cultural environments in a tone that is uncharacteristically bitter and direct for Senior. So, while the poem does not suggest a return to the aesthetic associated with Smith's era when 'land' *could* be celebrated, it is, it seems to me, haunted by nostalgia for that moment.

## GARDENS IN THE TROPICS

Another trajectory in Senior's engagement with nature focuses on the garden – that liminal horticultural space between 'Nature', with its associations of wilderness and 'Culture', with its associations of cultivated homeliness. 'Talking of Trees' takes a particular formal garden, Parade Gardens in Kingston, as its subject. Notes to the poem inform the reader that the Gardens, formerly known as Victoria Park and prior to that St William Grant Park, was a seven-acre piece of 'waste-land' which had been used as a parade ground for the British troops – and as a place for public hangings. Victoria Park was established between 1870 and 1871 when over 120 trees, including thirty-five different species, were planted and became a 'promenade gardens' for the colonial gentry to stroll in and to display their wealth and prestige. The notes indicate that the gardens were 'beautified' in the1980s and that most of the original trees are now gone.

In the poem the trees 'parade' their history, offering a schematic, fragmented, account of the history of the Park, and of Kingston. This includes references to the harsh realities of plantation slavery and resistance to it and to other historical moments: the earthquake of 1907, the arrival of the British troops. The trees appear here as witnesses whose rustling leaves tell (or 'talk') their own story:

> Su-su
> Su-su
> Su-su

> Once upon a time
> There were trees on Parade

> Trees on Parade?

> Trees on Parade. Listen:

> (*TT*: 80)

The conspiratorial opening lines invite the reader to participate in the gossip and story-telling: 'su-su', the Jamaican word for 'gossip', is followed by the familiar 'once upon a time' and the reader is told to 'listen'. The poem proceeds in irregular free verse stanzas, to offer fragmented glimpses of the trees' entanglement in Kingston's history: the 'fustic' tree which provides the yellow dye used to dye the soldiers' khaki uniforms; the above-the-ground roots of the mangroves which clog up the harbour ('Mangroves of resistance'); the hard 'Ironwood' which 'stains' the carpenter's life as he works the wood; and the banyan tree which provides a shady space for the 'Big-tree boys' to sit under to 'reason together'.

The poem shifts deftly from the focus on the spoken, with which the poem opens, to indicate a written history by referencing the rustle of leaves/pages in a book being turned, 'In Kingston some witnessed history/ Turn the leaves and see' (*TT*: 82). West Indian writers and political activists feature here

76

(W. Adolphe Roberts, the poet, and Vic Reid, the novelist, as well as Bustamante, the activist who organized workers in Kingston, following labour unrest in the 1930s). This stanza concludes with an irreverent reference to the monarch who would have presided over England and her colonies shortly after the Parade Gardens were established, 'Queen Victoria saw everything but is saving it for/ later' (*TT:* 83).

Botanical gardens of various degrees of elaborateness and complexity were established in many colonial locations and statues of Queen Victoria were a standard feature of many of them. Senior's notes include the comment that: 'Queen Victoria's statue since 1887 has been a resident of the park. The statue, recently moved to the eastern side, has so far faced three of the four cardinal points.' (*TT:* 86) It is not clear whether the statue was moved as a political statement, following independence, but Senior's ironic reference is clearly mocking in tone.[13] The poem also persistently undermines the very decorum and order which define formal gardens. Gardens were important sites in the colonial era, displaying 'proof' of Europeans' claims to proper care of the lands they appropriated and claimed as theirs. Botanical gardens, which brought together in one place plants and trees from far-flung colonies were also powerful signifiers of a commitment to scientific enquiry following on from exploration and conquest. They provided tangible evidence of European power and mobility: in addition to the millions of Africans transported as slaves, and Indians as indentured labourers, thousands of plants, trees and animals were also shipped. Jamaica Kincaid sees the methodical transplanting of trees and plants as part of a system of colonial control, intent on *demonstrating* its power to its colonial subjects: 'The botanical garden reinforced for me how powerful were the people who had conquered me; they could bring to me the botany of the world they owned. It wouldn't at all surprise me to learn that in Malaysia (or somewhere) was a botanical garden with no plants native to that place.'[14]

Senior, acutely aware of this colonial context, is careful in 'Talking of Trees' to note the origins of the trees, as well as the colonial origins of the Parade Gardens themselves. In the notes on the poem, a rueful comment on the bereft state of the Gardens in contemporary postcolonial Jamaica might be read as *both* nostalgia for the gardens in their more ordered state under colonial rule, and an oblique comment on the failure of postcolonial governments. It may also imply the incongruity of rehabilitating such colonial spaces for postcolonial uses at all. The poem's fragmented structure, uneven line-lengths and use of interspersed refrains comprised of the repetition of single words ('Strike/ Strike/ Strike/ Strike/ Strike'; 'baby/ baby/ baby/ baby/ baby') disperse the point of view and imply that the *who* and *how* of the telling is inextricably part of the drama of that history. In so doing, Senior implies a critique of the panoptical viewpoint characteristic of colonial grand narratives which the carefully regimented formality of Parade Gardens attempted to embody.

In *Gardening in the Tropics*, Senior returns to the motif of the garden but in these poems, the small-scale kitchen garden or provision plot provides the location for ruminations on history and other matters. The playful and lightly mocking use of 'tropics' in the title wryly gestures to the evocative resonances of this word ('tropical paradise' and so on). The twelve poems which comprise the 'Gardening in the Tropics' section are narrated by speakers deeply embedded *within* the 'tropical garden'. Senior explores ideas of 'working the land' that resonate with literal and metaphorical significations. 'Land' is again thoroughly imbricated in history so that the soil is represented as bearing the traces of human life over the centuries – which the poet must sift through and 'read' as she would an archive. Land, soil and earth in these poems are living, breathing archives of presences, ghosts, forgotten stories and distorted histories which the writer – as archivist/archaeologist – unearths and re-presents. To cite Glissant again, 'landscape is its own monument: its meaning can only be traced on the underside. It is all history'.[15] Senior's poems echo this approach as the gardener-poet 'unearths' fragments of stories, ranging over a broad historical frame, from the fateful first encounter of 1492 to the drug barons of contemporary Jamaica, eschewing strict chronology in favour of anachronistic associations.

The speakers in these poems, in keeping with the modest scale of their kitchen gardens, often speak in colloquial, coy and humble registers. This unassuming tone of voice is used to deliver a thoroughgoing critique of colonial and postcolonial abuses of the land and those who *work* that land. This tone is established in the opening lines of the first poem, 'Brief Lives':

> Gardening in the Tropics, you never know
> what you'll turn up. Quite often, bones.
> In some places they say when volcanoes
> erupt, they spew out dense and monumental
> as stones the skulls of *desaparecidos*
> – the disappeared ones. Mine is only
> a kitchen garden so I unearth just
> occasional skeletons.

(*GT:* 83)

The poem charts the unearthing of the remains of a young man, a victim of political rivalry, and wryly draws parallels between the humble re-burial in her kitchen garden that the speaker offers and the 'stunning funeral' of a drug baron:

> attended by everyone, especially
> the young girls famed for the vivacity
> of their dress, their short skirts and
> even briefer lives.

(*GT:* 83)

The modestly unassuming voice of the speaker, 'mine is only a kitchen garden', is deployed strategically by Senior to heighten the conspicuous materialism of the drug baron and his cohort and the transience of their lives.

In 'Seeing the Light', by contrast, attention shifts away from the immediacy of contemporary Jamaica to span some 500 years of misuse of the land. The poem catalogues the dramatic changes which colonization ('old' and 'new') inflicts on Caribbean lands in the name of 'progress', laying waste to the vegetation and forcing animals away. An image of modest, small-scale (and gracious) land-use by the Caribbean's first inhabitants provides a contrast:

> Before you came, it was dark in our garden,
> that's true. We cleared just enough for our huts
> and our pathways, opened a pinpoint in the canopy
> to let the sun through. We made the tiniest scratch
> on Mother Earth (begging her pardon). When we moved
> on, the jungle easily closed over the scar again.

(*GT:* 93)

The poem makes sustained use of the motif of 'light', including a rueful image of scattered 'pinpricks of light' to suggest the possibilities obliterated by the violence of the historical encounter:

> There was enough
> in the jungle to provide gardens for everyone.
> All over these green and tropical lands there
> could have been pinpricks of light filtering
> through the leaves to mirror the stars of Heaven,
> invert the Pleiades.

(GT: 94)

The speaker also questions the Christian narrative of God as bringer of 'true light' in a series of pointed questions:

> Why did those
> who speak of Light wear black, the colour
> of mourning? [...]
> Why on a dead tree did they nail the bringer
> Of light, one Cristo, torture and kill him
> Then ask us to come, bow and worship him?

(GT: 94)

Approval of the ethics of small-scale use of the land, historically associated with Amerindian cultures, is unequivocal here. But any temptation to read these questions as uncomplicated nostalgia for a pre-lapsarian innocence is undercut by the ironic title of the poem, 'Seeing the Light'. The colloquial associations of the phrase also work to domesticate the epic scale of the sweep of history considered in the poem. The discrete disruptions which titles and epigraphs can provide are frequently used by Senior to quietly dislodge expectations of various kinds.

Another poem, 'Gardening on the Run', again uses a colloquial phrase to frame the poem's larger historical theme. 'On the run', a phrase used in everyday parlance to refer to someone who has escaped from prison, adds contemporary resonances to the story of maroonage with which the poem is concerned. It draws on historical material on maroon societies to convey a sense of the desperation, persistence – and successes – of maroon struggles against enslavement. The poem opens with a runaway slave in Hispaniola but Senior's reconstruction shifts across other maroon communities, always alert to the significance of the story for the reader in the contemporary moment of reading. The poem lists the names of maroon leaders (Nanny, Cudjoe and Accompong) and the many spaces in which maroon slaves took refuge and eventually built communities, strong enough in some cases to force the English to sign treaties recognizing their autonomy. The speaker acknowledges the importance of environments that provide 'natural' spaces of refuge, punning on the meanings of the word 'plot' (as piece of land, as scheme and as narrative) in the process:

> Gardening in the Tropics for us
> meant a plot hatched quickly,
> hidden deep in forest or jungle,
> run to ground behind palisade or
> *palenque*, found in Cockpit, in
> *quilombo* or *cumbe*.

> (GT: 105)

The particular geography (mountains, thick forests, wide rivers) of the mainland territories of the Guianas (Dutch, French and British) as well as some of the islands, provided runaway slaves with spaces in which to hide. Here escaped slaves were free to express their spiritual and cultural beliefs and to establish a less combative relationship with the land than prevailed on the plantation. De Loughrey et al offer a reminder of this phenomenon:

> While the brutality of the plantation system produced a particular relationship to the natural world, it is important to consider those sites that served as vital repositories of indigenous and African beliefs and assertions of rebellion against plantation capitalism. This is most evident in the history of indigenous and slave resistance in which mountain ranges, mangrove swamps, provision grounds, and other sites of environmental opposition to the plantocracy provided vital alternative communities.[16]

Senior's poem alludes to this broad context, referencing words for maroon, 'quilombos' (used in Brazil, it derives from the Kimbundu language of modern-day Angola) and 'palenque' (a word of African-Spanish origin) to indicate the broad pan-African and pan-Caribbean significance of maroon history. The

81

poem also includes reference to Cockpit Country where maroons forced the British to sign a treaty in 1738.

The poem reiterates the importance of the maroon as a powerful symbol of resistance and includes an extract from an historical source, the trial of 'Copena and Claire', two slaves who ran away repeatedly in Western Cayenne (in what is now French Guiana). When they were finally captured, they were both sentenced to death, Claire by hanging at the gallows and Copena by a long tortuous death, which their children were forced to witness:

> *Copena, charged and convicted*
> *of marronage . . . is sentenced to*
> *having his arms, legs, thighs, and*
> *back broken on a scaffold to be erected*
> *in the Place du Port. He shall then*
> *be placed on a wheel, face toward*
> *the sky, to finish his days, and*
> *his corpse shall be exposed.*

(GT: 106)[17]

The display of the broken bodies of enslaved people was a routine spectacle of control on the plantation, an attempt to demonstrate to other slaves the futility of running away and the comprehensiveness of colonial technologies of control. Senior's poem foregrounds the impossibility of this quest for *absolute* control and instead draws attention to the proliferation of meanings these bodies-as-signs generate: defiance, dogged endurance and the will to be free. She suggests that the maroons' refusal to comply with the demands of the plantocracy, despite the violence with which such resistance was punished, confounds the plantation owners, their bafflement recorded in the excessive, obsessive *need to name* – 'runaway, maroon, cimarron'. The runaway's response, 'No matter what they called, I/ never answered' (*GT*: 105) conveys a stubborn refusal to be defined – and hints at the power of silence.

By including a fragment from an historical source in the poem itself, Senior requires the reader, too, to act as witness to the atrocities of colonial history – and to the ways that enslaved bodies haunt technologies of representation:

We are always there
like some dark stain in your
diaries and notebooks, your
letters, your court records,
your law books – as if we had
ambushed your pen.

(GT: 108)

The visceral image of the enslaved's body seeping into
documented history like a 'dark stain' evokes powerfully the
impossibility of suppressing those stories (and bodies) which are
so intimately bound up together in Caribbean history. This
connection is consolidated in the final section of the poem,
narrated from a more settled contemporary moment:

... Now I have
time to read (and garden), I who
spent so many years in disquiet,
living in fear of discovery,
am amazed to discover, Colonist,
it was *you* who feared *me*. Or
rather, my audacity.

(GT: 108)

The speaker concludes, with some bafflement, by noting the
perversity of the colonizer's obsession with re-enslaving the
maroon, 'for you saw me/ out there as your own unguarded/
self, running free' (GT: 108). The poem offers glimpses into
maroon history but, in also providing nuanced reflections on the
representation and significance of that history, it moves beyond
the more familiar registers of 'recrimination and despair', to use
Walcott's terms.[18] And again, the garden figures as both
repository of past presences and as a space that allows for
rumination and reflection.

In other poems, Senior uses the phrase, 'Gardening in the
Tropics' as a more playful pretext for traversing the land to
revisit and rewrite historical moments and mythical figures.
'Amazon Women', for example, opens:

Gardening in the Tropics, sometimes
you come across these strong Amazon
women striding across our lands –

(GT: 95)

83

The speaker invokes powerful mythological women figures (the warriors, Toeyza and Anacaona of the Worishiana and Taino respectively, and Nanny of the maroons) to draw parallels with the strength of 'ordinary' women' who perform their daily labours in the contemporary Caribbean. In celebrating the self-reliance, bravery and resilience of these women, Senior also implies powerful connections between Amerindian women and the African-Jamaican leader, Nanny. In so doing, she quietly affirms an *indigenous* lineage of feminism embedded in Amerindian myths, rather than in 'the West' that foregrounds connections between women of African and Amerindian origins. The obviously feminist agenda of the poem is mediated by the speaker's tone which is coyly dissembling, simultaneously declaring *and* disavowing its challenge to the reader:

> But
> you see my trial! I'm here gossiping
> about things I never meant to air
> for nobody could say I'm into
> scandal.
> .   .   .   .   .   .   .
> ...I hadn't meant
> to tell tall tale or repeat exotic
> story for that's not my style.
> But we all have to make a living
> And there's no gain in telling stories
> About ordinary men and women.

> (*GT*: 96–7)

The speaker appeals directly to the reader, deploying wit and humour to encourage the sense that the views being expressed are widely held, familiar and uncontentious. This device is consolidated by the use of bracketed asides which also invoke a shared cultural terrain, '(you know how men stay!)'(*GT*: 95), or '(though/ I'm not sure I would want my girl/ raised by a band of women outlaws/ keeping company with jaguars)' (*GT*: 96). This strategic use of 'respectability' is a recurring method throughout Senior's poetry.

A similarly understated, coy tone of voice characterizes the final poem, 'Advice and Devices', in 'Gardening in the Tropics'. Senior's choice of 'gossip' as the discursive register in this poem (as in 'Amazon Women', and others), suggests a mistrust of more overtly political or ideologically definitive registers of public speech. 'Advice and Devices' is narrated by a woman whose prowess as a gardener regularly earns her prizes at agricultural fairs and this prompts her to offer a series of tips on how to get the best from the land. The gist of this advice is to avoid the pesticides and fertilizers as well as the single-crop cultivation promoted by 'the government man/ with the book', treat the earth with respect and make use of the store of widely held beliefs and customs which the poem includes (plant Overlook Bean at the four corners of a plot of land, ask a pregnant woman to walk over the pumpkin vine, and so on), rather than dismissing them as 'old wives' tales' (GT: 111). This affirmation of small-scale, mixed agricultural land-use links this speaker to the Amerindian subjects of 'Seeing the Light' who also live in harmony with the natural environment. It is this approach to agriculture, she declares, which makes her crops 'put out their best' and gives her the confidence to assert:

> When they ask me for my tips,
> I take a deep breath and come
> right out and say: Just Live Right
> and Do Good, my way.

> (GT: 112)

The quietly playful, 'my way' in this final line introduces a note of knowing self-irony and undercuts the apparent 'righteous-ness' in the preceding lines. The careful management of small plots of land for growing provisions was a crucial feature of slave survival, allowing modest but steady improvements to their daily life. The centrality of the kitchen garden in these poems suggests continuities with that history.

In Senior's poems the natural environment, the earth and the garden provide multiple possibilities for the poet: an archival resource, a symbol of continuity with the past, a site of intense contestation as well as of tentative ideas of settlement and contentment. Rather than engaging with 'the land' as a monumental entity, Senior tends towards a more modest and small-scale approach, one that domesticates abstractions of 'history' and 'geography'. 'Gardening', in Senior's loose defini-tion, provides time and space and the kinds of activities that allow for contemplation and reflection, important antidotes to

85

the rapacious demands of both colonial exploitation and 'modern' intensive, mono-crop farming alike. In this way, Senior's interest in ecological matters, her 'eco-poetics' if you will, provides an interesting point of intersection with – and deviation from – writers such as Wilson Harris and Edouard Glissant who are most closely associated with a poetics aligned to the environment. Wilson Harris has written repeatedly of his sense of the landscape as a living entity pulsating with the traces of many geographies, histories and cultures. In 'Age of the Imagination', he argues that there is no 'firm and irreconcilable barrier between person and environment'; instead he sees the environment as 'a measure of reflection in the person, a measure of the cosmos in the person'.[19] Senior's poems frequently resonate with this sense of the permeability of the conventionally bounded worlds of 'human', 'animal' and 'mineral'. But, where Harris tends to represent this interconnectedness of humans and their environment in texts characterized by ontological and philosophical abstraction, Senior favours a more explicitly 'down to earth' approach. The colloquial register identified in the discussion above clearly contributes to this but her preference for anchoring reflections in the everyday world of the kitchen garden and in objects, or fragments, haphazardly 'found' also provides a sense of accessing 'History' via the ordinary, the small-scale and the domestic. In 'To My Arawak Grandmother', for example, 'Baptismal certificates are mute/ while the whisper of a clay fragment moves me to attempt this connection' (*TT*: 11).

Edouard Glissant provides another resonant reference point in relation to Senior's work. In *Poetics of Relation* he argues for a new relationship with the land, suggesting that 'the massacre of the Indians' renders any quest to find the true '"possessors"' of the archipelago futile: 'But the consequences of European expansion (extermination of the Pre-Columbians, importation of new populations) is precisely what forms the basis for a new relationship with the land: not the absolute ontological possession regarded as sacred *but the complicity of relation.*'[20] Mobilizing a metaphor from nature, Glissant proposes an emphasis on the rhizome: rather than the vertical, singular root of the arboreal, the rhizome suggests possibilities for multiple, horizontal and trans-species growths. Senior's 'gardening poems' might be read as performing the very 'complicity of relation' which Glissant heralds. She emphasizes chaotic entanglements rather than the singular or hierarchical, though in a more 'minor' or cautious key than Glissant's poetics implies. She is also careful not to reiterate the narrative of extinction that characterizes so many Caribbean references to indigenous populations; where Glissant speaks of 'extermination of the Pre-Columbians', Senior 'listens' to an Arawak clay fragment. Senior also remains alert to the ambivalent meanings of hybridity; 'The Knot Garden', opens with an image that celebrates the hybridizing impulses of the natural:

> Gardening in the Tropics,
> you'll find things that don't
> belong together often intertwine
> all mixed up in this amazing fecundity.
> We grow as convoluted as the vine.
>
> (GT: 86)

But 'this amazing fecundity' is rendered more complicated as the poem maps this image onto human relationships and the tensely 'convoluted' relationships across class boundaries that characterize an unnamed postcolonial state. Here, drug barons and unscrupulous political leaders share an 'anything-goes' language of profiteering which compromises the more celebratory idea of hybridity. The convoluted vine as a metaphor for social mobility in this poem does not signal a 'happy hybridity' but an *opportunistic*, materialistic mobility fuelled by greed.

Jordon Stouck discusses *Gardening in the Tropics* in relation to these ideas of hybridity and to questions of rootedness and mobility:

> Senior deploys these tangled histories to locate the Caribbean garden as a source of identity, a self-constituting memory, and, in its multifaceted colonial history and current global exploitation, as the (literal) root of her speaker's dispossession. This insistence on a continuing legacy of oppression usefully qualifies celebratory theories of the rhizome as a process of exchange and suggests that the way forward lies in exploiting the dynamics of belonging and exclusion, possibility and loss.[21]

Stouck argues persuasively that the tropical garden in Senior's work signifies in multiple and *ambivalent* ways, shifting between the garden as a space in which identity might be rooted *and* a space from which identity might be questioned and re-routed. Embeddedness in the soil does not represent a secure, rooted identity in Senior's poems but provides a space for reflection and for momentary respite from the vicissitudes of history. In 'Plants', Senior playfully draws attention to 'the colonizing ambitions of hitchhiking/ burrs on your sweater, surf-riding nuts/ bobbing on ocean, parachuting seeds' (*GT*: 61) to question the idea that 'plant identity' itself is *exclusively* one of 'rootedness' and fixity. If hybridity and creolization involve an idea of 'mix-up, mix-up' (as the village of Mount Rose is described, *ASW*: 13), then Senior's approach to this 'mixing' is one that suggests a very *cautious* welcome; it perhaps invites a critical response that must itself be 'mix-up, mix-up', rather than simply celebratory. To conclude this discussion of Senior's handling of 'Nature', I turn now to poems in which she thematizes the sea, an element that is the supposed antithesis of 'rootedness' and which has always been a rich resource, in metaphoric and practical terms for Caribbean subjects.

## 'THE SEA IS HISTORY'

The sea and the Caribbean littoral have always been – and remain – central to poetic evocations of the region. Derek Walcott's poem, 'The Sea is History' is frequently cited as exemplifying the centrality of the sea to Caribbean subjects: the Atlantic Ocean as Middle Passage, as burial ground for numberless, nameless slaves; and as that expanse which continues, of necessity, to be crossed by Caribbean subjects in search of work and/or better living conditions. In Walcott's poem, the sea 'holds' history:

> Where are your monuments, your battles, martyrs?
> Where is your tribal memory? Sirs,
> in that grey vault. The sea. The sea
> has locked them up. The sea is History.[22]

As Senior reads the soil as archival resource, Walcott reads the sea as a resource that might be made to 'deliver up' the not-yet-spoken of Caribbean history. In Edward Kamau Brathwaite's celebrated trilogy, *The Arrivants*, the endless journeyings of the black Caribbean man across the Atlantic are documented, sometimes angrily, often mournfully:

> Ever seen
> a man
> travel more
> seen more
> lands
> than this poor
> land-
> less, harbour-
> less spade?[23]

Walcott and Brathwaite, undoubtedly the most widely recognized of the region's foundational poets, engage intimately with the sea as perhaps *the* definitive element in Caribbean history and in shaping the region's aesthetic sensibility. But though both poets emphasize the ocean crossings as emblematic of Caribbean realities, they both in their distinct ways, also inscribe a return to the islands, a homecoming that is often presented as a necessary antidote to the perpetual crossings the poems chart. By contrast, Paul Gilroy's *The Black Atlantic,* published in 1993, might perhaps be seen as consolidating (if not inaugurating) a shift *away* from the pull of homeland and the certainties of nationalism. The emphasis on mobility and flux that characterizes Gilroy's 'Black Atlantic' paradigm continues to be a powerful strand within postcolonial discourse in ways that often render 'the local' and 'the located' as retrogressive or problematically nostalgic. Olive Senior's work intersects with these concerns in interesting ways: though her affirmation of local Jamaican/Caribbean realities are everywhere evident, her poetry implies connections across spatial and temporal boundaries in subtle ways (as I have argued above) so that 'the local' becomes imbricated in broader global concerns, blurring the boundary between 'local/global' and 'now/then'.

In an interview, Senior describes the impact of seeing the 'incredible turquoise' of the sea for the first time when, as a child, she was taken from her home in the mountains to Montego Bay.[24] Few of her poems focus on the beauty of the sea, dwelling instead on the sea as an expanse marked by a series of urgent, perilous and painful 'crossings'.[25] The figures who travel in Senior's poems include illegal immigrants, stowaways, migrants in search of work and those risking perilous seas to escape the harsh realities of life on the islands. These more humble travellers are discussed in detail in the following chapter. Here I look at those poems in which Senior considers a more privileged idea of 'the traveller', those associated with ideas of discovery, exploration and colonial privilege. The characteristically understated wit and tone of Senior's approach to *both* the historically insignificant *and* the historically momentous offers a productive point of comparison to the more dramatic tone of the poems by Walcott and Brathwaite referenced above. A short poem in *Shell*, 'CANOE/OCEAN'[26] is indicative here: the speaker declines to do more than let her/his net make 'a little scratch' on the ocean's surface, preferring not to intrude into the songs of the drowned. The poem concludes, 'I will just humbly take a little fish here/ and try not to upset' (*Shell*: 25). The reference to 'canoe' quietly invokes an indigenous sailing craft, rather than the bigger sailing vessels associated with the 'triangular trade'. In 'Message in a Bottle', the speaker expresses utter weariness, on behalf of the ocean with the quality of the writing contained in the messages and imagines the ocean praying for the invention of some other form of communication, 'postcards, telephones, E-mail,/ transatlantic cables' (*ORW*: 46). 'The Song that it Sings' invokes the endless 'keening', 'sighs', 'sadness' and 'whispers' associated with the sea (presumably the Atlantic) while also offering an 'ode to silver' inspired by the sea in moonlight. The typing 'mistake' that results in 'worldless' rather than 'wordless' playfully conveys a *universally* recognizable sense of *ennui* alongside an expression of the migrant's yearning for 'home':

> so far from the sea I find myself
> worldless. (Oh, leave it alone, but I meant
> to write 'wordless.') And sometimes, like
>
> tonight, I feel a hemispheric sadness: the
> New World as tired as the rest.

(Shell: 28)

In *Over the Roofs of the World*, Senior offers a more sustained exploration of what might well be considered *the* foundational voyage story of the region: Columbus's voyage of 1492. The collection takes its title from a phrase in Walt Whitman's poem,

'Song of Myself': 'I too am not a bit tamed, I too am untranslatable/ I sound my barbaric yawp over the roofs of the world'.[27] In doing so, Senior invites a loose association to be made with her American 'New World' predecessor whose breathless delight in himself and in the (natural) world she pays homage to – but also deviates from in the more understated tone and more deliberately modest reach of her own work. In 'The Pull of Birds', with which *Over the Roofs of the World* opens, a disorientated Columbus wonders 'where was Japan?' and prays 'for a miracle to centre him/ in that unmarked immensity as warp to woof.'(*ORW*: 9) A flock of birds flying south appears to him to be that miraculous compass:

> At such an auspicious conjunction, his charts
>     he threw out, the flocks drew him south
>                 across the blue fabric of the Atlantic
>                                (*ORW*: 9)

And so Columbus 'finds' the 'West Indies'. And Senior establishes the context for the playfully entitled section, 'A Little Bird Told Me . . .' which follows, taking a variety of birds (but particularly the parrot) as pretexts for a series of insights, secrets and mischievous revelations. This shift to a more colloquial register undermines the heroics attendant on accounts of that historical voyage. The use of the colloquial expression, 'a little bird told me', implies a speaker who does not want to reveal her sources of information but who makes other people's business *her* business. In other words, Senior again deploys the register of gossip in 'setting up' the poems, suggesting that 'the everyday', folklore and superstitious beliefs all contribute to knowledge and an understanding of the world – contrary to what 'History' may say. The most sustained attention is given to the parrot whose mythical significance and aptitude for mimicking human speech has made it a central figure in many castaway narratives.

'The Secret of Crusoe's Parrot', offers a sustained exploration of parrot's historical association with narratives of island-castaways that have in various ways powerfully impacted on Caribbean literature. While the title and several references in the poem declare their intertextual relationship with Defoe's *Robinson Crusoe*, many phrases in the body of the poem also echo lines from Shakespeare's *The Tempest*. Both these canonical texts have become key postcolonial texts as writers from colonized nations have read/re-read these narratives as emblematic of the encounter between the New World and the Old with all the violent power imbalances and unequal cultural exchanges that that entailed. Senior's 'The Secret of Crusoe's Parrot' charts parrot's relationships with the various humans who arrive on the island, drawing parallels with the 'Caliban' and 'Poll' figures, of both *The Tempest* and *Robinson Crusoe*. The second stanza plays on a line spoken by Shakespeare's Caliban, 'This island's mine, by Sycorax my mother,/ Which thou tak'st from me.' (Act 1 Scene 2) Here it is adapted to read, 'This island kingdom was Parrot's from time immemorial' (*ORW*: 18) and it is noted that, had Crusoe thought to *ask*, Parrot like Caliban could have revealed where the fresh springs on the island were. In the fourteenth stanza, mimicking (and deflating) Caliban's threat of miscegenation,[28] parrot reflects wryly:

> I had thought of peopling the island with educated parrots
>     and sweet airs. But I laid off the teaching
>         when I found I could no longer stand
>
> their screeching.
>
> (*ORW*: 19)

Throughout the poem, Parrot is presented as, like Anansi, 'playing fool to catch wise' (*ORW*: 18). Attuned to the self-aggrandizing of the men who seek to control the island and its occupants, parrot strategically 'plays dumb', while also recognizing the powerful lure of *speech*: 'I cannot stave off the yearning/ that will master me for words addictive as grain cracked open/ on the tongue.' (*ORW*: 19–20)

The island-as-Eden is a recurring motif in English literature. As Edmonds and Smith note, 'European voyagers until recently often thought of islands in terms of paradise or utopia, either an ideal inhabited island or else an empty island on which to start again.'[29] In 'The Secret of Crusoe's Parrot', Senior picks her way through the well-worn literary terrain of island and castaway motifs with ingenuity and wit. *The Tempest* and *Robinson Crusoe* have informed Caribbean writing in powerful ways. Two examples will suffice to indicate this: in *The Pleasures of Exile*, George Lamming offers an extended reading of the figure of

92

Caliban as paradigm of the colonized native subject and of that subject's ambivalent and fraught relationship with the colonial master and his culture. Derek Walcott deploys the poetic resonances of the castaway in many poems, inscribing the castaway as an Adamic, name-giving figure capable of inventing new words for the 'new world':

> We were blest with a virginal, unpainted world
> With Adam's task of giving things their names[30]

In Walcott's 'Crusoe's Journal' he cites lines from *Robinson Crusoe* as an epigraph before beginning his own exploration of the poetic possibilities of the island and horizon, 'from shipwreck, hewing a prose/ as odorous as raw wood to the adze'. And in 'Crusoe's Island', he celebrates the Friday's progeny:

> Now Friday's progeny,
> The brood of Crusoe's slave,
> Black little girls in pink
> Organdy, crinolines,
> Walk in their air of glory
> Beside a breaking wave;
> Below their feet the surf
> Hisses like tambourines.[31]

Postcolonial theorists have also taken up the implications of the Caliban/Prospero dynamic, especially as they relate to questions of 'native' agency and culture. Homi Bhabha's essay, 'Of Mimicry and Man', perhaps the most widely read of these critical interventions, argues that in the process of mimicking European colonial culture (as the colonized subject was required to do), the native unsettles the authority of that culture as *mimicry* slides into *menace*.

> The discourse of mimicry is constructed around an ambivalence; in order to be effective, mimicry must continually produce its slippage, its excess, its difference. The authority of that mode of colonial discourse that I have called mimicry is therefore stricken by an indeterminacy: mimicry emerges as the representation of a difference that is itself a process of disavowal.[32]

Senior takes a different tack to Bhabha and emphasizes the *mimicker*, rather than the culturally authoritative culture being mimicked and suggests an idea of mimicry that is, inevitably, promiscuously, complicit with the culture being mimicked. By extension, Senior implies that there is no 'clean' position from which the writer can resist this culture; there is only the entangled 'mix-up, mix-up' of the culturally and textually hybrid contemporary moment of writing. A brief comparison with Senior's contemporary, Jamaica Kincaid, is useful here. Kincaid declares her rage with the stark facts of her own postcolonial reality, writing *after* 1492 and *in* 'the language of the criminal who committed the crime': 'But nothing can erase my rage – not an apology, not a large sum of money, not the death of the criminal – for this wrong can never be put right, and only the impossible can make me still: can a way be found to make what happened not have happened?'[33] Senior's work makes use of a different strategy; cunningly using a strategically respectable voice, she insinuates her voice into these canonical texts so that they resonate subtly with a different presence and voice.

In such an overdetermined discursive context, Senior weaves a cunningly playful strand of her own into the field. She revisits and revises her canonical precursors (European *and* Caribbean) and inserts a colloquial, ironic register to infuse the text with her distinctive, cunningly deflationary wit. In the process of doing so, she defuses some of the 'sting' of the Caliban/castaway relationship as the defining paradigm of the colonial encounter. Given the definitiveness of Lamming, Walcott and Bhabha's exposition of the Caliban/castaway mimic man, it is difficult not to read Senior's intervention as a quietly mocking subversion of the male-centredness of this discourse, even as the poem (inevitably) reinscribes the symbolic power and romance of 'the European castaway'.

Senior's engagement with the natural world is central to her poetic rendering of the region. Caribbean land and sea are permeated by the violence of colonial history. As Senior notes in an interview, 'Columbus arrived and the first thing he did was set dogs on the Tainos. Our history, our written history, is born out of violence.'[34] Senior's deployment of various tropes of nature and of the poet as gardener/archivist suggests the ongoing imperative to fill in the gaps of the region's history pre-1492, even if what is missing can only be guessed at, mourned for, and retrieved tentatively in fragmentary form. 'Nature' functions not as backdrop to the drama of human lives but as a player in that drama. It is a resource that humans exploit and from which they can learn as well as be delighted by. But Senior also presents Caribbean land and sea as environments in which humans have always had to struggle to make a living, whether in the forests of South America, working on the harsh plantations, cutting the Panama Canal, reaping fruit on farms in the USA, making dangerous sea crossings in search of better opportunities, or serving in the tourist industry. It is to these labouring figures that the next chapter turns as I discuss the way Senior represents labour and craft of various kinds in the 'extraordinary ordinariness' of Caribbean lives that she documents.

# 5

# Spinning a Yarn: Labouring Lives, Migration Stories and the Writer's Craft

> Spinning a yarn is Olive Senior's stock in trade, whether in poetry or prose.[1]

So far I have discussed Senior's short stories and poetry in discretely separate chapters where the thematic concerns of the respective genres have leant themselves to such treatment. The short stories already discussed have a more tightly circum-scribed focus on Jamaican socio-cultural realities and tend to be written in a largely naturalistic mode while the poems offer a broader sweep of history, deploy more densely metaphoric registers and afford a more nuanced range of perspectives. These distinctions fit well with the familiar conventions associated with the short story and poetry respectively but there are many texts in Senior's oeuvre which sit less discretely within these categories and, as Anne Collett suggests, 'spinning a yarn' is something that characterizes Senior's work *across* genres. 'Spinning a yarn' also suggests an alignment between writing and weaving, a connection that Senior often makes and extends to embrace other kinds of 'craft', to embed the hard graft of writing in the context of other kinds of labour. This chapter begins with a discussion of texts in which labouring lives are the explicit focus, before shifting to Senior's use of story-telling as survival strategy for Caribbean subjects and for the poet herself as she articulates, via a weave of intertexts, her role as writer.

The plantation system defined enslaved subjects brutally in terms of their labour. In a sequence of poems grouped under the title, 'Shell Shock', Senior offers incisive glimpses into the harsh conditions on the cane fields. The speaker in 'Cane Gang' comments on the bitter irony of a system in which idyllic place names ('Eden, Golden Vale, Friendship, Green Valley') and the careful geometric order of the cane fields mocks the servitude and 'broken-down/ bodies' of those whose labour makes this order and fecundity possible (*Shell*: 51). In 'West India Cane Piece 1821', a slave working in the cane-fields compares his life to that of the rat, better only except for his own belief in an 'afterlife':

> For I know that if I'm careful and I eat no salt,
> If I don't mek Massa limb me, if I hold on to mi head
> If I sing King Zambi song while I live in this here prison,
> the minute that I'm dead, I fly straight back to Guinea.

> (*Shell:* 54)

In 'Shell Blow', Senior references the conch shell, a large shell which when blown into emits a distinctive sound. It was used to mark the division of time into units of labour on the plantation and used also as a call to prayer, and to acknowledge births and deaths and other events. She extends the conch's repertoire as medium of communication by invoking it as a repository of History, of stories which need to be disseminated and passed on. 'Shell' also describes the hard shell encasing the sweet flesh of the ripe sugar-cane. The sequence of poems with which *Shell* concludes, 'Empty Shell', by contrast, excavates the profound lack of humanity of those who amassed great wealth from the plantations and from the labour of those they enslaved. The excessive consumption of material goods is presented in stark contrast to the dearth of spiritual and cultural values of the indolent plantation owner. 'The Poetics of a West India Dinner Party *(mid-seventeenth century)*' makes the case dramatically by simply listing the vast array of foodstuffs on the evening's menu, 'Taken word for word (and arranged "poetically")', the poet's note informs us, from an historical source (*Shell*: 81). The conspicuous consumption indicated in this list of rich foods is left to speak for itself in context of the many poems alongside it that evoke the lack of sustenance, of any kind, afforded the enslaved. Another author's note informs us that the shell motif for the collection, was inspired by a visit to Fonthill Abbey, built by William Beckford Jr., whose considerable wealth came from his family's slave plantations in Jamaica. Nothing now remains of 'Beckford's folly', a fact Senior deftly exploits to convey the lack of humanity animating such acquisitive attitudes, what she refers to in 'Auction' as 'the poetics of possession' (*Shell*: 86). Where the emphasis in 'Shell Blow' is on the need for the formerly enslaved to remember and re-tell stories, in 'Empty Shell' the *glut* of information on the accumulation of wealth, housed in prestigious libraries, itself becomes oppressive

> And nothing
> can stave off the relentless grinding down by
> this new slavery: the collections, the recordings,
> the writing of history.

> (*Shell*: 92)

Documented History here is an inescapable *burden*, inflected by the uncannily unsettling presence of those dominated *by* that History so that 'the master' finds 'each letter, ant-like, running together/ in a black connecting trail. A coffle. A sentence.' (*Shell*: 85) As in *Gardening in the Tropics* and *Over the Roofs of the World*, Senior takes a particular 'natural' motif, here a shell, and turns it around and examines it from diverse perspectives (zooming in and panning out), and in many registers (wry, angry, resigned, understated, declamatory), to multiply the metaphoric possibilities of seemingly commonplace objects or phenomena. This polyphonic poetics encourages an equally nimble reading as the reader is invited to look at historical events from several perspectives within one poem. Slavery and its (long) historical legacy continues to define Caribbean culture and writing. Senior's distinctive contribution to this collective 're-memorying' is to offer the reader modulated and nuanced points of entry into this 'unspeakable' story, to glimpse some of its truths as they continue to resonate.[2]

The end of slavery did not signal the end of exploitative work regimes and Senior's writing repeatedly bears witness to this history. While not often the *explicit* focus, her short stories are populated by figures (male and female) that work hard on the land to support their families or are forced to search for work abroad to make a living. Whether it is small-scale banana farming (the father in 'Ballad'), seasonal farm work in Florida (the eponymous 'Ascot'), work in Colon (Dev in 'Window' or Lily in 'Lily, Lily') or never-ending domestic chores (in numerous stories), hard labour continues to be a defining feature of Senior's representation of Jamaican life. In recent decades, the quest for employment has intensified as the withdrawal of preferential agricultural trade arrangements with the UK (as the former colonial power) combined with punitive International Monetary Fund policies have impacted heavily on poorer Jamaicans. Stories such as 'Country of the One Eye God' (SL) and 'The Lizardy Man and his Lady' (DH) convey a sense of the violent impact of this impoverished context on contemporary Jamaicans, particularly men. Senior's contemporary, Honor Ford Smith, outlines the harsh socio-economic realities that force so many Caribbean subjects to leave the region in search of work. She argues:

> This migration is not a matter of individual choice: it is a systematic response of millions to the social and economic reality of a region that increasingly functions as a kind of Bantustan. By that I mean that the region produces labour for export across borders, and functions as a kind of impoverished holding area for labour that it is unable to employ.[3]

## MIGRATION STORIES

A people on the move/ Always on the move[4]

Many of Senior's poems explore the circumstances that have made migration such a defining feature of Caribbean life. The opening section of Gardening in the Tropics entitled 'Travellers' Tales', opens with a series of 'Hurricane stories', each associated with a particular year (1903, 1944, 1951, 1988) that explore the impact of hurricanes on people who have little to buffer them from such events. In 'Hurricane Story 1903' a child tells the story of the family's survival thanks to the wisdom and prudence of the grandparents who have of necessity, gathered knowledge of 'all the ways of orchestrating disaster' (GT: 20). The daily necessity of dealing with a harsh natural environment is presented here as instilling a matter-of-fact survivalism as well as respect for the elements and a quiet confidence in dealing with its vicissitudes. The idea of travel in 'Hurricane Story 1944' concerns movement across and 'down' class lines: the father, a 'white-collar class' 'dandy' marries a girl 'who don't come from nowhere' (GT: 24) and who will, his family fears, cause him to 'turn down'. The father loses his respectable job when 'Solomon's Drygoods and Haberdashery' is demolished by the hurricane and refuses to return to 'rooting/ in the soil' (GT: 26), forcing the family to rely on the mother's labour on the land and her earnings as a higgler.[5] The final stanza describes the family's new routine:

> Monday Tuesday Wednesday our mother worked in the fields
> Thursday Friday she went to market
> Saturday she left him money on the dresser
> He took it and went to Unity Bar and Grocery got drunk
> came home and beat her
> Sunday she went to church and sang

> (GT: 27)

The matter-of-fact tone of delivery here conveys the repetitiveness of the cycle of drudgery of the mother's life and parallels her matter-of-fact response in taking on the role of breadwinner for the household *and* the punishment for doing so. The poem also, of course, provides an updating of the familiar children's rhyme, 'Soloman Grundy'.[6]

The hurricane which prompts a young couple to migrate, in 'Hurricane Story 1951', allows the poet to narrate an almost archetypal Caribbean migration story. Margaret goes to England to study nursing but ends up working as a hospital cleaner; she decides, beaten by the harsh realities of her life in England, not to contact the son she leaves behind in Jamaica, waiting 'until she could send him/ what amounted to/ something' (GT: 35). Delbert goes to America to work on the orange farms, eventually achieves some economic success, remarries and sends for their son. The boy, deemed 'too hard-ears' (disobedient) is left to his own devices in America and withdraws completely from language, spending his time on the shoreline throwing 'sounds across/ the ocean' (GT: 37):

> Every day now

> Ah-o
> Ah-o

100

Ah

Till one day
He managed:
Ah-o
Ah-o
Ma-

(*GT*: 38)

The boy's mother eventually 'hears' and recognizes these sounds as she sluices the floor of a hospital in Reading. She strips off her clothes and wades to meet them through the 'ocean' of water she throws from her slop pail, as the hospital staff rush to restrain her. The poem ends with the son, in turn, hearing his mother's faltering words '- my son/ my s –' and he starts 'walking/ to meet it' (*GT*: 41). What begins as a migration love story of this 'fine young couple' (*GT*: 34), full of possibilities, ends with an image where both movement and sound are suspended; communication between mother and son in this metaphorical Atlantic Ocean crossing is left pending, neither refused nor delivered but *promised*. Like the mythologized story of the enslaved Ibos who after landing in America, turned round and walked into the sea, heading back to Africa,[7] Senior's narrative poem inscribes the symbolic resonances of imagined connections where harsh circumstances prevent it. The poem's ending resonates with the tragedy of the story just recounted (with its implications of distress if not 'madness' on both sides of the Atlantic) but it also insists on a powerful reality-defying investment in spiritual connections and crossings. The poem, in other words, demands to be read as an account of both the crushing *and* the resurgence of spirit.

Set at a time when large numbers of West Indians were being recruited to work in Britain,[8] 'Hurricane Story 1951' painstakingly outlines the losses and traumas which migration entails: the fracturing of relationships, the erosion of dreams, the undermining of self-esteem. It works against the grain of the current tendency within a range of critical discourses, including migration, diaspora and postcolonial discourses, to celebrate migration and the figure of the migrant. Alison Donnell, offers a persuasive discussion of the way Senior (and others) challenge the prevailing acceptance of a Black Atlantic paradigm with its emphasis on hybrid forms, fluidity and movement. She concludes:

> In a critical moment in which the states of in-betweenness, migration and exile have accrued value through postcolonial theorizations to the point where dislocation is regarded almost as a virtue in itself, Senior's writing helps us to explore what it means for those people who have to stay, who choose to stay, or for whom moving on is not moving up.[9]

Certainly, the poems in 'Travellers' Tales' emphasize the hardships and dangers of perilous crossings and the anguish about loved ones left behind (see 'Illegal Immigrant' and 'Stowaway', for example). 'Caribbean Basin Initiative' offers a sustained exploration of the travails of a group attempting to escape an unidentified island and cross the waters to America. The poem's title refers to the Reagan administration's initiative to ally US trade interests with those of the Caribbean to consolidate free market practices and intensify the USA's economic advantage in the region. The failure of these policies has been well documented and its impact on the fragile postcolonial economies of the Caribbean has been devastating, intensifying the pressure to migrate. The poem highlights the initiative but also desperation of these would-be migrants in embarking on, and surviving, the hazardous crossing. In Senior's typically lightly allusive style, no direct reference is made in the poem itself to the 'Caribbean Basin Initiative' though American power is clearly and bitterly referenced in the sixth section of the poem when the remaining passengers are 'reclaimed' and deposited on Guantanamo:

> No mariners here.
> Here there be
> Marines.
> Yes, Sir!

> (GT: 332)

Instead of articulating any direct political commentary, Senior leaves the title of the poem, 'Caribbean Basin Initiative', to do the work and trusts the reader to flesh out the implications. (In the quote above, there is also of course a reference to Coleridge's 'The Ancient Mariner'.) The epigraph to this poem is deployed in a similarly allusive manner. It reads:

102

'The canoes being small...the water lapped over the edge in an alarming way. Had any of us sneezed we must have foundered.' – Mary Kingsley: *Travels in West Africa*, 1897 (*GT*: 29)

As she does with the title, Senior simply suggests a context with which the reader is expected to be familiar (or to familiarize herself with). Mary Kingsley's position as a *woman* traveller was remarkable but her class and cultural privilege as a European ensured that she travelled in comfort, in direct contrast to the desperation and life-threatening circumstances of those described in the poem itself. Kingsley's account of her travels in West Africa fall into the genre of travel writing associated with the colonial enterprise in which European travellers assume a knowing and authoritative perspective on 'their' colonial subjects. The epigraph and title together imply historical continuities between the Victorian colonial moment in which Kingsley wrote and the twentieth-century imperial ambitions of the USA under Reagan. It is the disastrous consequences of such colonial continuities for the poor that the poem narrates. The first stanza of the poem conveys this vulnerability in terms that are both moving and understated. In contrast to the epigraph's rhetoric of alarm and self-dramatization, there are no big heroics here:

> Like limpets we cling
> on craft
> that ply
> in these waters
> where our dreams lie.

(*GT*: 29)

After describing the speaker's abortive journey, internment at Guantanamo and eventual deportation, the poem concludes by repeating the first stanza (though 'we cling' now becomes 'we'll cling'), attesting to the ongoing and dogged persistence of the surviving passengers. The words 'boatpeople' and 'refugee', which perhaps inevitably shadow this poem, are strategically avoided so that the circumstances the poem dramatizes elude recuperation in the familiarly sensational register of journalism. Although the political context is clearly invoked, in the title and epigraph and in the reference to Guantanamo and so on, Senior's focus is on the human impact of these political circumstances, in the detail of *how* they are experienced.

An early poem, 'Searching for Grandfather', provides another example of Senior's method of engaging with the drama of migration history. The moment of migration here predates the well-known migration of West Indians to Britain in the 1950s to focus on those who travelled to help build the Panama Canal. It is estimated that between 1904 when work on the Panama Canal was started by the US and 1914 when it was completed, 25,000 West Indians migrated to Panama in search of work. Many thousands of labourers died in the harsh working conditions there making 'the cut' at Culebra which divided the continent, a crucial stage in linking the Atlantic and Pacific oceans. In addition to the hard labour involved, the fatigue and illnesses (malaria was particularly rife), black labourers were treated in decisively discriminatory ways. A two-tiered pay system was implemented: the Gold and Silver Roll system which ensured that white workers were paid in gold while black labourers were paid in silver (black workers became known as 'the silver people') and accommodation and other social and health benefits were similarly differential. In Senior's poem, detailed references to the specific history of labour on the Panama Canal anchor it clearly in that history but these references are minimal so that the emphasis remains on its impact on one individual, the grandfather:

> Along the Line I found my
> Grandfather disconnected
> at Culebra.
> Hacking at the Cut

(*TT*: 12)

Following a bout of malaria, he returns home with 'his fortune intact:/ Twenty-eight dollars and two/ cents. Silver.' When he dies, 'there was nothing left of the/ Silver Roll to weigh down his/ eyes.' Senior incorporates recognizable historical facts into the fabric of the life she is searching for *and* imagining into being in the poem. The harsh ironies of History are often conveyed wryly as when the speaker notes that the paucity of his 'fortune' in 'Silver' means there is nothing to weigh down his eyes.

In 'The Case Against the Queen' (*DH*), migration is presented in similarly compromised terms. The story is narrated by Girlie, who, orphaned at birth, lives with her grandparents. When her

104

uncle returns home after spending twenty years 'studying' in England, Girlie is his only confidante; the fact that no one is sure what he was studying, suggests that he may well be doing manual labour. 'Uncle Sonny' returns home without any of the symbols of success and gifts from abroad that his parents had expected, 'It wasn't that they really wanted anything. It was a matter of principle; they needed things to show off with. Just like everybody else.' (*DH*: 46) On his return, their son is silent and introverted, his days punctuated by the rigid routine of his daily walk at 4 in the afternoon, dressed in three-piece suit and bowler hat and stepping out with his walking stick as if onto a Piccadilly Circus pavement and not a village path. With his ramrod stiff gait and precise pace, he reminds Girlie of a wind-up, mechanical toy. The mother explains her son's strange behaviour as a direct consequence of his time abroad where all the studying he has done has caused 'brain strain' (*DH*: 46), 'Is studiration bring him to this' (*DH*: 54). The father concurs tersely:

> Lawd, woman, is foreign mad him, [...] We send off a good-good boy to England dress in him suit and tie, looking like a little Englishman before him even reach. Is them place mash him up. People not suppose to go so far from home. It weaken yu constitution. You nuh see how much people round here gone mad from foreign? (*DH*: 48–9)

The explanation Uncle Sonny offers Girlie might be read as his own *literal* interpretation of what his parents can only guess at. He says that while in England he was forcibly hospitalized and that Her Majesty the Queen's doctors attached wires to his head, removed his heart and replaced it with a mechanical one. The scale of compensation that Uncle Sonny demands (six million pounds) and his analysis of the reasons for his hospitalization (that he and others like him have been reduced to providers of labour) invite connections with the larger brutality of slavery and with contemporary arguments about reparation: 'Because those people only understand machines. That's what I found out about them. Want to turn us all into machines. So they can work us as they like and wear us down as they like and nobody can say one little thing. *Because we are not human any more.*' (*DH*: 53, my emphasis) Having presented Uncle

105

Sonny as eccentric, if not 'mad', Senior gives this character one of the most strident declamations of anti-colonial sentiment in her prose; 'madness' perhaps allows the unspeakable to be spoken powerfully here.

Migration is again presented as a painful experience for those who migrate *and* those who remain at home. Uncle Sonny returns home a 'mechanical man', doggedly maintaining the dress and demeanour of an English gentleman, despite his absolute certainty that England has damaged him irreparably. He simultaneously mimics *and* challenges 'Englishness' even as he is devastated by his inability to be recognized in England as fully human, however 'gentlemanly' his behaviour. Senior's version of mimicry suggests a complicatedly ambivalent process that works to alienate Uncle Sonny both at home and in 'foreign'. In this narrative, the intersecting stories of Uncle Sonny and Girlie's migrations to England offer more quietly suggestive conclusions to one of the questions posed in Salman Rushdie's *The Satanic Verses*: 'how does newness enter the world?' Rushdie's protagonists, Chamcha and Gibreel, are jettisoned from a jumbo jet over the English Channel and as the two men flail around in the sky, the narrator asks:

> How does newness come into the world? How is it born?
> Of what fusions, translations, conjoinings is it made?
> How does it survive, extreme and dangerous as it is? What compromises, what deals, what betrayals of its secret nature must it make to stave off the wrecking crew, the exterminating angel, the guillotine?[10]

The energy, high drama and multiple possibilities that characterize Rushdie's handling of migration in *The Satanic Verses* (and other of his texts) is often embraced as being representative of the experience of migration. In this scenario, although the figure of the migrant is associated with loss and pain, he/she is also presented as bursting with agency, creativity and a capacity for mutation and transformation.

Senior takes a more low-key approach, suggesting that contemporary migrations are themselves not 'new' but inflected by longer histories of migrations. Her stories also imply that the ties which bind migrants to the stories, places and people left behind are impossible to shake off. So, parallels are established between Girlie's later experience of studying in England and those of her Uncle when she notes: 'From England, I wrote nothing but good news to Gran, but I fretted and prayed for my own sanity, for at times I caught a glimpse of what might have happened to Uncle.' (*DH*: 54) Girlie's experience of metropolitan London is at least partially filtered through the template of her Uncle's experiences in the city, so that 'the old' inflects her apprehension of 'the new'. Girlie's determination to provide 'nothing but good news' suggests that she has learnt lessons from her grandparents' disappointment at the lack of good news and/or gifts when Sonny was abroad. But it also suggests that she intuits the almost talismanic power of repeatedly naming her experiences in London as 'successful'. Her return home as a qualified doctor provides the catalyst for Uncle to begin to unpack his trunk of papers and 'pour[ed] out his presence' (*DH*: 56), and perhaps abandon his 'case against the queen'. Together, these criss-crossing movements between 'home' and 'foreign' and across the generations allow migration and the migrant subject a degree of agency that hinges on *both* 'here' and 'there', the local and the global.

Rather than the more familiar focus on the 'newness' that emerges within metropolitan contexts with the arrival of migrants, Senior implies a continuous to-ing and fro-ing between 'home' and the metropolis. This approach foregrounds the integral part played by migration in the Caribbean for centuries, rather than emphasising the most recent experiences of migrancy as characteristic of modern (or postmodern) subjectivity. Rather than deploying characteristically postmodern narrative strategies of suspending temporalities and histories in the chaos and dynamism of the present, Senior tracks particular histories and locations as distinct but intersecting times and spaces. In this way, the detail of small stories interrupt or 'snag' the (grand) narrative of global migratory movements as dramatically transformative. The new, in other words, is always already old.

## HARD GRAFT – AND HARD CRAFT

I want to turn now to poems that make the hard labour – and

107

craft – of those who stay at home their subject. Here, as with the migration narratives, the poems provide more explicit commentary on these subjects than do the stories, though the latter, too, are populated by people whose everyday existence is defined by and depends on hard labour. In *Gardening in the Tropics*, the connection between working on the land and working poems out of the land implied an organic relationship between gardening and writing. It also suggested strong historical continuities between the diverse relationships to the land that this poetic trajectory charted – perhaps most explicitly in 'Meditation on Yellow' with its list of 'labouring verbs': slaving, loading, peeling, toiling, chopping, mining, cane-rowing and so on. In *Shell*, the violent historical entanglements of those who worked the land and those who owned it were the main focus. In *Over the Roofs of the World*, Senior develops a connection between another kind of labour, that of weaving, embroidering and sewing. Traditionally associated with women working in domestic rather than commercial spaces, Senior's handling suggests more complex and contradictory associations with this 'feminine occupation'. Grouped in the last section of the collection entitled, 'Penny Reel', the poems revolve around the needlework/textile motif (apart from 'Pearl Diver', which catalogues the grim daily routine of a 15th-century pearl diver).

'Penny Reel', focuses on the Maypole Dance, derived from the European maypole dance and, as the notes indicate 'popular in bygone days in the colonies' (*ORW*: 105) when each dancer paid a penny for a turn at plaiting and unplaiting the ribbons. The poem opens:

> It is Saturday, the night of penny reel dances. Girls in
> pressed hair, white muslin and sashes, turn to
> high-stepping gentlemen as they weave out and in
> eye passing each other on the go-round.

*(OWR: 80)*

While the young people dance ('Freed/ from labour, from tenement rooms, they abandon themselves to each other', *ORW*: 82), the dressmaker sits in *her* tenement room sewing through the night to complete the dresses ordered for church on Sunday. Her thoughts, punctuated by references to the penny reel she knows the others are enjoying, circle and spool around the

108

children she must work to feed, the man who bullies and grinds her down and the customers who pay her late (if at all) – 'Do they know/ she is coming unstitched?' (*ORW*: 81) The sewing which keeps her feet moving on the treadle also provides the metaphors and images which shape the woman's world-view and her place in that world, 'Who decides on our measure?/ She addresses this to no one in particular.' (*ORW*: 80) The poem concludes with the woman 'needling' the abusive man with her eyes and imagining that the thread she knots and bites off the finished garment is a noose around his neck. The routine labour the woman performs at her sewing machine also allows her space for reflection (in a manner reminiscent of Senior's 'tropical gardener') and she imagines herself transcending the reality of the daily grind: 'Not the straight-stitcher looking after/ the children but the one overlooking':

> The one
> who rips her skin, strips and discards it, so that
> bat-like, taking wing, she flies through the air,
> homing only to sound, to movement, the scent
>
> of the dancers O my sisters who are reeling. She dives
> for their blood. To suck up their being.

(ORW: 82)

Here, the dressmaker embraces her man's abusive description of her as an Ol'Higue[11] and becomes the voracious monster in a fantasy of revenge. The escapist scenario is disrupted by the sound of the revellers returning home at dawn and she is 'grounded' again. In this poem, labour defines and confines the woman: the sewing machine keeps the woman anchored while others are at play but sewing also, claustrophobically, provides the images of rebellion and transcendence, albeit illusory and self-destructive.

The woman making lace in 'Lacemaker' entertains similarly murderous thoughts as she 'grow[s] brittle and dry' and her eyesight becomes 'opalescent as shell' from all the fine needle-work she has to do, trimming the ruffs, cuffs and albs of her Lord and Lady's clothing with lace. Subtitled, 'Valenciennes, 1794,'[12] the poem invokes the cataclysmic historical drama of the French Revolution by focusing on an individual 'peasant' whose life has been spent labouring for the powerful. The closing lines suggest both a promise of rebellion and deflated resignation:

> Meantime, the spider and I wait
> for our traps to be sprung
> for lace-trimmed heads
> to swing in bloodied air
>
> (What a waste
> of good lace
>
> What a waste
> of my lifetime).

(ORW: 86–7)

Senior also suggests wider affiliations for social justice (across time and place) by transplanting the cunning spider (Anansi) to the context of a subaltern subject in France. In 'Lacemaker' and 'Penny Reel', Senior also exposes a menacing underside to conventional perceptions of needlework as 'woman's work', requiring 'nimble hands' and painstaking, patient labour. The poems lament the relentless toil required of some subjects, suggesting that the lace and clothing generated by such toil are inevitably tainted by the exploitative circumstances in which they were produced. But the poems also challenge the idea of 'feminine passivity' which has, since Penelope, been associated with women sewing. In 'Embroidery', the women in the family who *do* sit around sewing, do so while gossiping and 'bad-talking' those in the family whose 'difference' makes them suspect; the speaker responds to this conclusively, 'I [...] became a blue foot traveller. /Kept no diary. Sewed up my mouth. Shunned embroidery' (ORW: 79).

'Basketmaker' and 'White' foreground the skill and craft involved in basket-making and laundering respectively. The note to 'Basketmaker' describes the belief of the Warao (of South America) that the level of their craft and skills in life assures them of a special place in the after-life. The poem invokes this belief, acknowledging the skill involved in basket-making but also suggesting the organic connection between the maker and the object. 'White' focuses on a laundress whose work bleaching and cleaning clothes is rendered in explicitly metaphoric terms at the outset through the epigraph, '*Take me and make me whiter than snow*' taken from a Protestant hymn (ORW: 83–5). The opening lines establish the understated irony that prevails throughout, 'Nothing comes white here naturally, not unless/ you count sea foam . . .'; the frequent references to 'you' implies a generic 'one' or 'I' but the tone also suggests a listener/reader being hailed. When coupled with its chatty register, this irony positions the poem at the interface between a dramatic monologue and a more conventional poetic internal reflection. This choice of voice has interesting implications for the relationship between the *speaking* subject of the poem and the subject *about whom* she/he speaks. The first stanza's ironic literalizing of the Christian narrative of spiritual redemption as a whitening process ends with the words, 'Try telling that to Miss Dora'. The speaker then describes the way Miss Dora beats the clothes into submission and starches them so stiffly that no breeze could possibly 'come tek fass and undress them'. The washed and starched clothes hang on the line 'like flags, in glorious array like cherubim and/ seraphim, though Miss Dora don't have business with that' (*ORW*: 83). The washerwoman is completely un-persuaded by the speaker's description of a heaven where sins are washed away and skin is whitened. Miss Dora does not go to church: Sunday really *is* a day of rest as it is her day off work. Heaven, for Miss Dora, 'is the day I retire/ from the work and put up my feet' (*ORW*: 84).

'White' cleverly suggests a dialogue between the laundress and someone in the household over the meanings of the word 'white': its metaphoric significance in Christian ideology, as in the epigraph, is of spiritual goodness. Senior's speaker tries to persuade Miss Dora of the metaphoric resonances of 'white', 'is skin we talking about./ If sin wash away in Heaven sinners come whiter/ than snow.' Miss Dora resolutely refuses the language of metaphor (of Heaven, she says, ('Hm. Never seen') and insists on what she *knows*, such that the down-to-earth job of washing clothes delivers the significance of 'white' and 'clean'. But Senior's cunningly ironic handling of these positions and voices unsettles a reading of this poem as a stand-off between the pious Christianity of the householder and its refusal by the washerwoman whose work ethic implies a better value system. For colonial deployment of Christianity *did* cohere around a very literal mapping of spirituality onto 'white' subjects so that the speaker's understanding that 'is skin we talking about' *does* embody a *literal* truth – a strategically important one for those seeking upward social mobility. Miss Dora uses the language of the here-and-now, of her labour, as the grounds from which to oppose what she recognizes as a *deceitful* culture of metaphor. The poem presents it as a deliberate rhetorical strategy, a tactic emphasized in the concluding stanza when Miss Dora voices her reservations about the dubious aesthetic appeal of white skin.

> ...If ever I should arrive at
> them high-up place there, as a good washer
> woman I couldn't hold mi tongue, I would
> duty bound to say, Lord, I glad I reach but I have
> to beg you Sar, please go easy on the bleach.

(*ORW*: 85)

Senior's cunning handling of voices and positions makes the distinction between voices – of the poet, the speaker and the spoken *about* – slippery and hard to separate. All these positions and voices are partially truthful and partially complicit, but always knowing. Senior makes modulated use of Jamaican Creole throughout the poem to suggest a *convergence* of voices and subjectivities that sets up a continuum of poetic possibilities that shifts easily between the parameters of the *performed* Jamaican Creole of, say, Bennett's work and the highly *poeticized* Jamaican Creole of poets like Lorna Goodison and others. Senior does not speak *for* or *as* the washerwoman here (as is the case in Bennett's dramatic monologues) but weaves the various voices together so that they resonate against and through each other. In other words, Senior frequently threads the interpretation and incisive commentary of 'ordinary' working people alongside more obviously reflective and declarative poetic registers. In so doing, she extends the weave of intertexts that inform her work as a writer so that it includes the everyday and ordinary alongside allusions to literary and historical sources.

## ONCE UPON A TIME: STORIES TO LIVE BY

The story-telling which characterizes everyday life is a central feature of Senior's Caribbean. 'Nansi 'Tory' comments directly on the power of story-telling, for both teller and listener, and suggests the kind of *work* that stories can do. It tells the story of an African man 'brought as cargo' in the hold of a ship to the New World. He brings with him only 'his shit/seed/ and a bagful of memory' leaving his heart behind near the slave trading post of Elmina, Ghana. The poem registers the bitter counterpoint between the luxuriant growth of new plants and the man's deathly existence:

> Landing
> they emptied the hold
>
> where the shit fell
> grew luxuriantly
> fruits of Africa/New World
> akye, aloe, adrue and
> compellance weed
>
> the man
> they sold
> (Sweet sugar cane/sweet
> remembrance)
>
> For the rest of
> his life
> he was sure
> he had died
>
> (TT: 28–9)

It is not until he is prompted by the persistent questioning of a child that the man finally opens his 'bagful of memory' and with the words 'Once upon a time' begins the restorative process of telling his story. The retrieval and affirmation of those aspects of African culture which slavery sought to obliterate is a recurrent theme in Caribbean writing; what is distinctive in Senior's affirmation is the wryly understated tone in which this affirmation is made. The stanza following the one cited above, for example, defuses some of the pathos of the circumstances by drawing attention to the artifice of story-telling, and of the possibilities for refusing 'reality' which this artifice allows. So, just as the man gives himself up for dead, the speaker announces:

> But since this
> is a story he
> grew up to be
> somebody's grandfather.

113

(*TT*: 29)

Story-telling, in all Senior's work, has the potential to heal and restore as well as to expose and critique. The role of the writer includes bearing witness for those whose lives and labour remain undocumented but the intertwining of the speaking voices of labourers that I have argued for here suggests a poet who also seeks to anchor her poetic labours (and voice) *within* this community of workers

## A CREOLE SPIDER-WORK OF MANY HANDS (*ORW*: 98)

In the final section of this chapter, I look at two poems that chart affiliations with the writer *as worker*. Senior's poetry is richly and widely intertextual; sometimes as in 'Pearl Diver' a literary quotation is riffed against playfully (it opens by 'tampering' with Shakespeare's *The Tempest*, 'Full fathom five/ - or ten, my father/ will dive', *ORW*: 88) while in others a dedication or a phrase is included to widen resonances. *Over the Roofs of the World*, for example, takes its title from Walt Whitman's 'Song of Myself' without acknowledgement. In 'Meditation on Red' and 'Ode to Pablo Neruda', there is sustained engagement with Jean Rhys and Pablo Neruda *as writers*. The intertextual relationships here are intimate and detailed as Senior playfully – and seriously – reflects on their work and the impact of that work on her own. The diverse meanings of the word 'craft' come into play: '**1.** Skill or ability, esp. in handiwork. **2.** Skill in deception and trickery; guile; cunning. **3.** An occupation or trade requiring special skill, esp. manual dexterity. **4.a.** the members of such a trade, regarded collectively. **b.** (*as modifier*): a *craft guild*. **5.** A single vessel, aircraft, or spacecraft.' (*Collins English Dictionary*, 1984: 348)

'Meditation on Red' is placed in the 'Travellers' Tales' section of *Gardening in the Tropics* where it extends the focus on the varied histories of Caribbean travellers to include artistic craft and writing itself as a mode of travel. The epigraph is taken from a letter written by Rhys and sent from Cheriton Fitzpaine, Devon where she lived for many years and where she is buried, 'I feel I've been here for...centuries. Even this winter dates from the dark ages.' (*GT*: 44) The poet-speaker, on a pilgrimage to Rhys's final resting place reflects on the sense of restlessness and 'unbelonging' that characterized Rhys's life, particularly the sense suggested in the epigraph of being 'entombed' in England, cut-off from the colour and vibrancy of life in the West Indies. The poem opens by directly addressing Rhys:

> You, voyager
> in the dark
> landlocked
> at land Boat Bungalows no 6
>
> (GT: 44)

The speaker hails Rhys in the name of one of her novels, *Voyage in the Dark*, and throughout the poem fragments from Rhys's fiction are quoted and letters and other biographical sources that emphasize Rhys's anxiety about the value of her literary output are woven into the poem. The detailed intertextual links accumulate to convey a powerful sense of a speaker-poet whose intimate engagement with Rhys's oeuvre is palpable throughout the poem.

The poem might be read primarily as an elegy for Jean Rhys but in Senior's handling the melancholic, lamenting tone that conventionally defines the elegy is accompanied by a more playful one as the speaker attempts to chivvy Rhys out of the grey moods that prevail in her accounts of life in England. The speaker-poet tacks deftly between Rhys's autobiographical and literary texts to offer an empathetic re-telling of the well-known drama of Rhys's life-story and literary reputation. So, for example, Rhys's well-known preference for red as a symbol of warmth and passion is referenced throughout the poem, as is her dismay with the relentless grey of England. The speaker-poet adds 'green' to this colour-coding in a gesture which seeks to free Rhys from the dramatic palette of red/grey:

> You (destiny:
> storm-tossed)
> never saw
> the rolling downs
> patchworked
> in emerald, peridot
> mint, celadon
>
> (GT: 44)

115

Later in the poem, the speaker notes Rhys's attempt to cheer herself up from the sense of being 'Marooned/ in the grey' by gardening and she quotes from one of her letters, 'I wanted heaps of poppies...Not one came up'. So, by way of compensation, the speaker declares, 'I've come to/ wake you/ with spring flowers'. (*GT*: 46–50) If 'gardening in England' defeats Rhys, the referencing of flowers (particularly those tropical flowers Rhys is known to have preferred, ' – flame of the forest/ hibiscus/ heliconia/ poinsettia/ firecracker/ bougainvillea–' (*GT*: 51) establishes a link between Rhys and the speaker of the poem and, within a collection entitled, *Gardening in the Tropics*, embeds Rhys within this 'tropical garden' as a more accommodating final resting place than the churchyard in Cheriton Fitzpaine.

The poem offers its homage to Rhys in several ways: in the journey the speaker makes to Rhys's grave; the flowers placed there in tribute; the photo taken to record the moment; the intimate acquaintance with Rhys's work evident in the many intertextual links; the use of a halting rhythm and fragmented sentences which convey the sense of interrupted, disjointed thought which is a feature of Rhys's work. But perhaps most fundamentally, this homage is consolidated in the insistence on Rhys's place as literary foremother for Caribbean writers:

> Right now
> I'm as divided
> as you were
> by that sea.
>
> But I'll
> be able to
> find my way
> home again
>
> for that craft
> you launched
> is so seaworthy
> tighter
> than you'd ever been
> dark voyagers
> like me
> can feel free
> to sail.

> That fire
> you lit
> our beacon
> to safe harbour
> in the islands.

(GT: 51–2)

The unequivocal assertion of this literary lineage is also consolidated in more subtle ways in the poem as, for example, where the speaker suggests that Rhys was '*Marooned*/ in the grey' (*GT*: 46, my emphasis). That Rhys was alert to the significance of the maroons in Dominica's history is clear in *Wide Sargasso Sea* and Senior endorses Rhys's 'right' to this emblem of Caribbean resistance. Further, by including exploration of Rhys's own experience of displacement and her writing *about* that displacement as part of the travels and travails of Caribbean people, Senior weaves Rhys tightly into the fabric of Caribbean culture. Rhys has not always been so readily accommodated within the canon of Caribbean literature where 'authentic' Caribbean identity has tended historically to exclude 'white' writers. E. K. Brathwaite states the case for her exclusion definitively when he argues: 'White Creoles in the English and French West Indies have separated themselves by too wide a gulf [...] to give credence to the notion that they can, given the present structure, meaningfully identify or be identified with the spiritual world on this side of the Sargasso Sea.'[13]

Interestingly, in an interview with Anna Rutherford in 1986 Senior makes this comment on Rhys's work:

> I find it hard to identify with most of Jean Rhys's work because it seems so alien from the Caribbean. Apart from *Wide Sargasso Sea* and now the autobiographical material, I don't know that there is a strong Caribbean element; it seems more European to me. The difference between her women and Caribbean women is that the latter group don't act as if they are victimized. They're very positive, no matter how poor they are. They're into struggle, whereas Jean Rhys's heroines give up very easily. (*SL*: 17)

Eight years after this interview in 'Meditation on Red', Senior revaluates Rhys's place in her own work and beyond to acknowledge the ways that 'struggle' *was* a defining feature of Rhys's work as a writer; her long years of struggling to get *Wide*

117

*Sargasso Sea* 'just right' are well documented in her letters and elsewhere. That Rhys also struggled with a profound sense of the way women's options in life were curtailed by patriarchy is clearly evident in her fictional and autobiographical texts, as is a recurring sense of being cut adrift from 'home'. The speaker in Senior's poem, addressing Rhys, says that she, too, is ' ... as divided/ as you were/ by that sea' (*GT*: 51) but then goes on to present Rhys's writing as the compass that can help her navigate her return.

'Travellers' Tales' opens with 'Meditation on Yellow' while 'Meditation on Red' is placed towards the end; the similarity of the titles, the extended length and organization of the two poems suggest that there are structural reasons for this. It strikes me that Senior is suggesting that the two meditations on 'yellow' and 'red' resonate against each other to affirm the importance of a broad spectrum of Caribbean histories: political, economic, cultural *and* literary. The poem concludes by insisting on the importance of Rhys's craft as literary anchor for the contemporary poet-speaker/speaker-poet and as enabling other 'dark voyagers' to speak. In so doing, it suggests a dual sense of homecoming: Rhys is welcomed back home to the Caribbean and the contemporary poet – figured within the poem as Senior herself – finds her anchor and home in Rhys's craft.

The final poem in *Over the Roofs of the World*, 'Ode to Pablo Neruda', offers another extended reflection on the skills, responsibilities and anxieties particular to the poet's vocation. As with 'Meditation on Red', Senior pays homage to a writer by engaging in a 'conversation' with that writer. In this case, she addresses Neruda by name and inscribes or 'nests' his words within her own poem. This intertextual intimacy, combined with the focus on the craft of poetry and the urgency of some of the questions posed, position the reader as eavesdropper to the poet's anxious self-interrogation. The poet-speaker declares early on in the poem that her ability to pay homage to Neruda is hampered by her location 'in the north', miles away from her own home – and his:

> separated by a continent from Santiago, Isla Negra,
> or my own island home, so far from the sea I can't strike
> the right chord; the measure that I tread moves no one else.
> I find myself drifting and wordless.

> (*ORW*: 92)

This distance from home which prompts the desire to pay homage in the first place compounds the anxiety about her perceived role as poet: 'away from the elements of which my life has been spun/ I can't even remember what the knot stands for/ that I'm feeling in the thread that fills my hand now' (ORW: 93). Taking up Neruda's idea of 'grasping poetry like thread', the poem goes on to explore the precarious nature of writing poetry:

What if I use it all up – for a clothesline that breaks,
for a leash the dog runs off with? What if there's no thread
left? And no more where it came from? There, I've said it.

(ORW: 93)

In the remaining seven sections of the poem, the speaker probes the diverse aspects of her role as poet, including her responsibility to those whose labour she benefits from now, and those ancestors and historical figures she inscribes in her work – as well as the ones 'lost' to the Atlantic that she can't name but whose presence she intuitively apprehends, 'like floating/ sargassos on the currents of life' (ORW: 99). Senior sustains the image of the 'thread of poetry' throughout, deploying the motif in moving as well as amusing ways. In the fourth section, for example, beginning with her own 'pearl of anxiety' (ORW: 98), she constructs a rosary comprised of beads which represent the whole gamut of Caribbean arrivants, from European convicts, cut-throats, rebels and patriots to African slaves drowned at sea or transplanted in the New World, to indentured labourers. Deployed in this way, Senior recuperates a religious talisman (the rosary) to her own ends and provides a powerful image of the figure of the poet worrying away at the beads of history:

A chain-link of miles strung out across oceans
a creole spider-work of many hands.
The beads telling not decades but centuries.

(ORW: 98)

In the process of charting these 'beads' of history, the speaker affirms a sense of belonging in the *world*, suggesting that the cathartic process of crafting the poem has itself restored a sense of belonging, one anchored in *craft*:

119

So much more unstated as my legacy. Not found in my
blood but possessing me. The fibres of belonging to this world.

(*ORW*: 100)

As in an earlier poem, 'To My Arawak Grandmother', poetry
provides a space in which Senior can declaim her refusal of
affiliations based on 'blood inheritance', 'My spirit ancestors are
those/ I *choose* to worship' (*TT*: 11, my emphasis). The obligations
and responsibility of this notion of belonging – to the world and
to the world of poetry – are serious and focused, extending
geographies of belonging beyond the (relatively) simpler
geography of 'homeland'.

But the poem relieves the intensity of this quest for belonging
in several places with unexpected and pleasingly light touches.
For example, in the sixth section of the poem, the speaker muses
on the connection between the 'weaving' of a poem and the
more conventionally 'feminine' occupation of sewing:

I wanted more than woman's knotted portion so I refused
to learn the way of thread: sewing, embroidery, darning,
weaving, tapestry, knitting of crochet do not appear on my CV.

(*ORW*: 101)[14]

In an earlier section, the speaker acknowledges wistfully that it's
fine to play cat's cradle and skip rope with 'the thread', 'But
there comes a time when you might be/ forced to confess: I don't
know what I did with the rest of it'. (*ORW*: 94) The weight of the
writer's obligation here is presented through a charmingly
childish register which amuses while also conveying a sense of
the palpable fear involved.

The poem is both a paean to Neruda and an interrogation
and exposition of the craft required to follow in his footsteps.
The weaving motif provides the structuring focus of the poem
but within that structure Senior fluently deploys a range of
registers of tone and mood so that, by the end of the poem,
there is a sense of the poet-speaker having demonstrated poetic
flexibility and the necessary, fine balance between responsibility
and pleasure:

And so, my trickster powers evolving, I'm learning like you,
Pablo Neruda veteran tightrope walker, to swing more easily
*between joy and obligation*

(*ORW*: 103)

"Ode to Pablo Neruda' charts the long apprenticeship, skill and work required of a poetic vocation. In doing so, it patiently aligns the labour of the poet with that of other labourers – those whose lives many of the poems in Senior's collections attempt to inscribe. Like 'Meditation on Red', 'Ode to Pablo Neruda' implies a writer whose craft involves hard graft *and* a crafty way with metaphors. These two poems acknowledge Senior's indebtedness to Rhys and Neruda in particular but her work is peppered with references to a wide range of literary texts and contexts which, when combined with the many voices of 'ordinary' Caribbeans in her work, embodies the very qualities the speaker sees in Neruda's work:

> A chain-link of miles strung out across oceans
> A creole spider-work of many hands.

> (*ORW*: 98)

I argued in Chapters 2 and 3 that Senior's stories offer insights into the everyday social realities of 'ordinary' Jamaican lives. The short story form allows Senior the amplitude to convey in some detail the concerns, worries and pressures involved in growing up and making a living in Jamaica. Senior works with the short story form in several ways, as we have seen. The poem in Senior's hands is often a small fragment – presented as if it has been stumbled upon, or simply 'found' before being examined through a poetic lens. Few of the poems make use of a regular rhyme scheme or evenly divided stanzas, relying on rhymes that occur mid-sentence and rhythms that build up slowly and quietly. Poetry appears to allow Senior a different kind of amplitude in terms of the registers of voice she deploys and the negotiations she makes between local and global concerns – and between stories and histories. The possibilities for the kind of self-reflexivity evident in poems such as 'Ode to Pablo Neruda' as well as the range of linguistic and emotional registers which Senior is able to deploy in her poetry offer nuanced and complex re-presentations of Jamaican/Caribbean landscapes and subjects. Poetry's eye/I, in short, is exceptionally well suited to Senior's penchant for the small-scale, the in-between and the fragment. In the following chapter I discuss Senior's work in yet another genre of writing, that of the cultural archive, particularly as it, too, engages with 'fragments' of Jamaican culture.

121

# 6

# The Writer as Cultural Archivist: Olive Senior's Non-Fiction Works

Up until 1989 when Senior left Jamaica, she worked in the field of communications and book publishing where she wrote articles and speeches, worked as a freelance editor and also edited two major Caribbean journals, *Social and Economic Studies* at the University of the West Indies (1972–7) and *Jamaica Journal* (1982–9) published by the Institute of Jamaica Publications. *Jamaica Journal*, in particular, was extremely influential in encouraging scholarship on Caribbean culture and in embedding the literary in these discussions. Senior has, indeed, made her living from writing as she states, 'my entire professional life has been spent either as a journalist or an editor'.[1] Her professional involvement in writing is extensive and varied and covers a considerable span of time. Her most recent non-fiction publication, *Encyclopedia of Jamaican Heritage*, published in 2004 took twenty years of research to complete. And, although her first collection of short stories was *published* in 1986, the stories were *written* in the mid-1960s and early 1970s.[2]

*Working Miracles: Women's Lives in the English-Speaking Caribbean*, which appeared in 1991 was one of the first texts to focus exclusively on the role of women in the Caribbean. It was also among the flurry of publications which challenged the prevailing tendency in the 1980s for feminist work to be associated largely with 'white western' women. This was consolidated in initiatives undertaken as part of the United Nations 'decade for women' (1976–85) by several publications which focused on 'non-western' women's lives. *Working Miracles* is part of this trajectory and also provided a welcome shift away from the prevailing male-bias in anthropological and sociological studies of the region. Edith Clarke's pioneering study of family structures in Jamaica, *My Mother Who Fathered Me*, published in 1957 drew attention to the powerful role of the Afro-Caribbean woman as head of at least one-third of all Caribbean households. The 'dominant' role of the Afro-Caribbean woman generated concerns about the 'marginal' role of men that this implied, spawning fears that men were put 'at risk' by women's relative successes and strengths. Senior's study addresses the contradictory position of the Caribbean woman that results from this context and offers a comprehensive account of women's roles and status within the region, using the various stages of the female life-cycle to structure the book. The book gathers together the research findings of several years which had been generated by the Women in the Caribbean Project (WICP) with a view to influencing policy-making concerning women. As Joycelin Massiah, Director of the Institute of Social and Economic Research (Eastern Caribbean) states in the foreword, although the WICP had begun to disseminate its findings: 'Yet there still remained a sense in which it was felt that the project findings were not reaching a wide enough cross-section of the societies. And so *Working Miracles* was born – *an attempt to translate the WICP findings and their meaning into clear, easily assimilated prose for the benefit of the general reader.*' (WM: xi–xii, my emphasis)

The commitment to accessibility that was a feature of much feminist work in the 1980s and 1990s is evident in Senior's text which draws on a wide range of sources and disciplines. The material used includes statistics, ethnographic, sociological and historical data as well as the life stories of individual women, some of which are often represented as direct speech in the text. The cover of the book includes an image of one of the Jamaican Edna Manley's sculptures and many other images of her sculptures feature in the book. Senior also draws on many literary texts throughout the book to help ground the discussion in tangible and evocative examples; the title of the book itself is taken from a poem by Lorna Goodison, 'My Mother', which celebrates the strength of the mother in 'making do'. The text patiently evaluates and 'unpacks' this image of the Caribbean woman as 'miracle-worker', offering evidence of the ways in which many women, particularly working-class women, *do* work miracles to keep their households functioning, whether it is going without food themselves or/and engaging in arduous labour of various kinds. But Senior also catalogues and questions the cost to the woman of *having to* play such a role and draws attention to the invisibility of the work women do to absorb the cost of economic policies in the region which have required radical restructuring of the economy, often in response to IMF dictates.

*Working Miracles* provides careful coverage of the many arenas in which girls and women are discriminated against in the region, whether in the family, educational institutions, the church, the workplace, in government or in relationships with men through marriage or more informal arrangements. Throughout the text, Senior grounds discussion of these issues in knowledge of the contexts in which women's opportunities and expectations are framed. So, for example, in evaluating the way that 'motherhood' continues to be a defining role for women in the Caribbean, even as it burdens them with responsibilities, Senior recognizes that: 'in the absence of other or better societal rewards, or alternative role models, it is in bearing and rearing children that most women play what they perceive as their most important role in life; they derive not only emotional satisfaction but power and authority from parenting.' (*WM*: 189)

Feminist theory informs her approach but is inflected by the *particular* circumstances that obtain in the Caribbean: the nuclear family is not taken as normative and other family formations, such as 'child sharing' are acknowledged. Senior discusses the contradictory attitudes to children which prevail in the Caribbean, where they are both loved and 'prized' as symbols of women's status but also disciplined harshly. The contradictions of women's attitudes to their own independence is also addressed: although women *do* make most decisions in the households they head, they also frequently expressed the view that it *looked better* if they appeared to defer to men in public situations, indicating a mixture of both complicity with their own oppression and cunning at resisting that oppression.

Many of the themes addressed in *Working Miracles* clearly

resonate with themes considered in the short stories and poems, as does the carefully understated feminist approach. Rather than equivocation in Senior's feminism, her approach to the systematic discrimination against women is acutely aware of the historical factors which have constituted the Caribbean and through which gender relations are inevitably refracted. From the perspective of the Caribbean, as well as other postcolonial locations, feminists have commented on the balancing act required to negotiate across the demands of nationalism and feminism. Senior's approach in *Working Miracles* goes some distance in refusing to read these ideologies as *necessarily* in opposition to each other. However, the fact that there is no discussion anywhere in *Working Miracles* of lesbianism as an alternative to heterosexual relationships might be read as an indication of the degree to which nationalism as a normatively *male* ideology, continues to define the parameters of feminist ideology in the region.

In the final chapter of *Working Miracles*, Senior expresses regret that the book has not been able to cover the kinds of cultural changes that characterize the contemporary Caribbean. She identifies these new phenomena as resulting from both the influence of 'foreign' cultures as well as indigenous forms of culture such as reggae and dub. I quote from this at length because it sets the context for the discussion of Senior's cultural archival work which follows:

> Caribbean societies in the last few decades have been caught up in world-wide changes and are probably more buffeted than most, given their smallness, openness and exposure to metropolitan culture, especially North American. Even in the most remote villages of the Caribbean there are overseas connections [...] Cinemas are *flooded* with foreign films and, in the absence of strong indigenous publishing, news stands are *flooded* with foreign publications. Because of the long historical significance of external migration and the influence of the mass media and tourism, a 'foreign' life style and mode of behaviour is widely admired and imitated, especially by the young. At the same time, the rise over the last few decades of a strong and assertive indigenous popular culture, manifested, for example, in reggae and 'dub', in a new breed of socially conscious calypsonians and in the widespread practice of Rastafarianism, must be taken into account. (*WM*: 193, my emphasis)

125

Although the citation above references indigenous forms that are also changing the cultural landscape of the Caribbean, the language deployed to describe the impact of 'foreign' culture on the region indicates considerable concern, if not alarm. Senior has expressed this concern directly in many interviews and it is woven into her fiction and poetry in a variety of ways, some more directly than others. Senior's work in researching and collating the *A–Z of Jamaican Heritage*, followed by the more comprehensive, *Encyclopedia of Jamaican Heritage*, might be read as an attempt to anchor Jamaican culture more firmly in *its own* indigenous cultural history in order to prevent it from being completely 'flooded' by foreign imports. Given her concern with the damaging impact of foreign culture on Jamaica, Senior is acutely aware of the irony of her own position as a writer living outside of Jamaica, 'a bluefoot traveller'[3] (*ORW*: 79): 'But I personally feel the need to give something back. And that is why I have spent the last twenty years of my life working on the *Encyclopedia of Jamaican Heritage*. Because in a way I say, okay, I'm part of the problem, and this is my way of giving back something.'[4] Senior's location overseas appears to intensify her engagement with and commitment to that which has been left behind. Paradoxically (perhaps), rootedness in the specifics of Jamaica's culture, landscape and people is affirmed from the author's location 'elsewhere'.

It is also interesting to consider the *purpose* of a text like *Encyclopedia of Jamaican Heritage*: who might wish – or need – to *consult* such a volume? The introduction to the *Encyclopedia* does not give a reason for compiling this information, simply assuming its necessity. It is taken for granted that the erosion of Jamaican culture by foreign imports of various kinds and the 'dying out' of old customs and traditions generates the need for this compilation. The introduction opens with a brief definition of 'heritage':

> For me, it is everything from the past (our inheritance) that shapes us and serves as pointers to who we are, both as individuals and a nation. This includes the good and the bad, the serious and the frivolous. Obviously, not all the elements in this book are known or shared by all Jamaicans; indeed they reflect our great diversity. (*EJH*: ix)

The terms used to group the entries under this idea of 'heritage' are 'place', 'creative activity', 'history', and 'rituals and traditions'. This is further organized in subject categories: 'the natural world', 'economic life', 'cultural activities', 'domestic and leisure activities', 'folklore', 'historic people', 'historic events' and 'historic places'. The text is 500 pages long, includes nearly 1,000 entries and 700 images. The individual entries are presented in alphabetical order starting with 'A' for 'abeng' (the animal horn used by maroons as a means of communication) and ending with 'Z' for 'Zouave' (referring to the Jamaica Military band whose 'Zouave' uniforms derive from the French colonial troops whose uniforms caught Queen Victoria's eye and so they were introduced into the British colonial regiment). The entries are as varied as the categories above would imply and range in length from a short paragaraph (on, say, 'galliwasp', a lizard invested with great significance) to several pages (on 'Taino' and 'slavery'). Each entry 'stands alone' and the whole text, in keeping with the genre of the encyclopedia, is clearly intended to be used as a reference book, rather than as a seamless account of Jamaica's cultural heritage. This arrangement results in interesting and unlikely juxtapositions as diverse cultural practices, historical moments, key figures, and various flora and fauna jostle eclectically in the text.

It also results in an inadvertent 'textual democracy' as entries are arranged according to the 'chance' of the alphabet, rather than any other cataloguing principle or hierarchy. Thus, popular cultural practices sit alongside big historical events, images of Taino pottery resonate against those of contemporary Jamaican sculptures and entries on 'Indian' and 'Irish' (documenting the distinct but significant circumstances of their respective arrivals in Jamaica) are separated by a page. The (re)presentation of fragments of cultural life which results from this arrangement is suggestive. Senior herself notes that: 'For me, breaking down complex information and reassembling it in this fashion (alphabetically) opened up new connections and facets of experience and provided fresh perspectives on many of the subjects contained herein.' (*EJH*: x)

Perhaps, thinking back to Senior's comments, cited earlier in this study, that Caribbean people 'represent the coming together of fragments of people bringing fragments of their cultures with them',[5] the *Encyclopedia* represents an *ideal* genre to encapsulate the region's culture? This is not an entirely frivolous suggestion; certainly Senior is acutely aware of the difficulties of offering a truly *representative* account of Jamaica's heritage, given its diversity. The *Encyclopedia*, because of its non-linear structure, allows the disparate, disjunctive pieces of the many complicated stories of the region's people to resonate against each other to produce *glimpses* rather than a *picture* of Jamaica's heritage. After outlining the main 'ethnic categories' of Jamaica, Senior argues in the introduction that: 'We are not newly minted and fashionably "multicultural". We have been the meeting ground, from our earliest history, the coming together of peoples (and their cultural baggage) from all over the world.' (*EJH*: ix) Here, an interesting distinction is implied between diasporic or 'multicultural' migrant populations in metropolitan contexts and those in Jamaica who all share, in varying degrees, a volatile and often violent history of arrival. As in many of the poems (particularly the 'Hurricane Story' sequence), Senior's interest in migration tends to follow a longer historical trajectory, facing 'backwards' in time and to the Caribbean region itself, rather than embracing the contemporary, global and 'fashionably multicultural' idea of migration and diaspora. In acknowledging that 'not all the elements in this book are known or shared by all Jamaicans,' and that 'Jamaica as a nation is a recent invention' (*EJH*: ix) Senior is also acknowledging that the *Encyclopedia* is both documenting Jamaica's heritage as well as contributing to the *construction* of an idea of Jamaican heritage itself as a cultural resource. Her creative engagement with the various archival sources she draws upon and the sheer scale of the project – involving twenty years of research – indicate clearly her commitment both to finding what constitutes Jamaica's heritage and *extending* the definition of that heritage.

One of the distinctive features of the *Encyclopedia* is the breadth of coverage it offers, drawing on an extensive range of scholarship across many disciplines from both oral and scribal resources. All encyclopaedias are intrinsically intertextual and this one is no different: Senior acknowledges the written sources she consulted to produce the various entries but also notes that, 'Some of the basic information regarding Jamaica's traditional culture is based on my personal knowledge or from interviews I have conducted over the years.' (*EJH*: x) The text incorporates an eclectic range of intertextual relationships and inscribes the oral, the popular and the everyday as intrinsic dimensions of Jamaica's heritage. An encyclopedia is also intertextual in terms of how it is *read*, in that readers often consult an encylopedia in relation to a query generated by a different text or context. The dynamic interleaving of texts and contexts associated with the production *and* reception of an encyclopedia such as *EJH* is particularly suggestive in a postcolonial context where information about 'the native' and 'native culture' as well as the position of the 'native informant' have come under intense scrutiny. One of the texts that launched postcolonial studies as a distinct field of study, Edward Said's *Orientalism*, drew attention to the distorted knowledge about 'the Orient' produced by non-native 'orientalist specialists'. Writing after Said, Gayatri Chakravorty Spivak has repeatedly warned of the complications involved for both the native *and* non-native scholar who seeks to provide 'better knowledge' about the native (or subaltern) subject. How might the 'information' about native culture provided in Senior's *Encyclopedia* be located in relation to these broadly defined concerns, as well as in relation to the more immediate concerns about a 'national culture' in Jamaica?

At first glance, the idea of collating and preserving 'Jamaican heritage' may appear to be inherently conservative. After all, as many postcolonial scholars have argued, cultural identity – national or individual – cannot simply be excavated from the past but is always imagined or invented in relation to a particular set of factors at any given cultural moment. It is, in other words, not simply a matter of following lines of inheritance (as if that were ever simple) but also about *contingencies*, choices made, and paths taken. Debates about cultural inheritance have been central to the Caribbean, a region where most of the population comes from elsewhere and where the only 'truly' indigenous peoples (Amerindians) now exist in drastically reduced numbers and have relatively little say in cultural politics. In this context it is not surprising that quests for 'cultural roots' have often focused on 'finding' a line of inheritance that is pristine and uncontaminated by European culture. It is perhaps also not surprising, as I argued in the first

129

chapter of this book, that this route to roots has often generated an emphasis on oral and popular cultural forms of the kind Senior is keen to document.

James Clifford offers persuasive insights into these issues in 'On Ethnographic Allegory'. He argues that thinking about 'the oral' as a pristine space of authentic indigeneity implies a degree of nostalgia for what the West has 'lost'. The oral here is fetishized and functions as a version of the pastoral, distinguishing 'the rest' from 'the west'. In Clifford's argument the ethnographer or anthropologist then functions (problematically) as a subject-with-agency who can rescue that which has been lost (oral culture) – by writing it down. Clifford then rehearses 'a parable' in which a student conducting field research in Gabon on the Mpongwe conducts an interview with the current Chief. The researcher draws up his interview questions about Mpongwe customs after consulting a compendium of local customs compiled in the early twentieth century by a Gabonese Christian ethnographer, the Abbé Raponda-Walker. At some point during the interview, the Chief is puzzled by a question from the researcher about a particular word: '"Just a moment," he says cheerfully, and disappears into his house to return with a copy of Raponda-Walker's compendium. For the rest of the interview the book lies open on his lap.'[6] Although Clifford's explicit focus is the ethnographer in the field, I find his re-telling of this 'parable' suggestive in that it draws attention to the flux and dynamism of *all* contemporary cultures, and to the impossibility of maintaining the boundedness of the oral and the scribal, a blurring of boundaries that Senior's texts repeatedly thematize. He argues:

'Suddenly cultural data cease to move smoothly from oral performance into descriptive writing. Now data also move from text to text, inscription becomes transcription. Both informant and researcher are readers and *re-writers* of a cultural invention.'[7] Bearing Clifford's arguments in mind, I would argue that the *Encyclopedia of Jamaican Heritage* resists the lure of nostalgia for 'folkways' by being as inclusive as possible and by asserting the *equal* importance of both the oral and the scribal. Senior explicitly acknowledges her debts to both the oral and the scribal arenas at a personal level: 'For, although I soon claimed the world of books or it claimed me, my first primer was the natural world of Jamaica, my first teachers the sometimes unlettered folk who were nevertheless capable of "reading" the world around them in sight, sound, colour, gesture, meaning, utility and relationship to mankind.' (*EJH*: vii)

In other words, Senior is anxious to indicate at the outset of the *Encyclopedia* that her conception of 'reading' as an interpretive process is not exclusively tied to books and that this looser concept of 'reading' might provide a bridge between the worlds of oral and scribal cultures. This is reiterated towards the end of her short introduction where she expresses the hope that readers might share the insight and pleasure she derived, as author, from the eclectic juxtaposition of entries: 'Then "heritage" might be seen not as something exclusively encoded in great houses or the arts of one set of people, but as that to which each of us can lay some claim.' (*EJH*: x)

The particular circumstances of Senior's life have clearly positioned her well to mediate between the worlds of print and speech (better perhaps than the unnamed ethnographer in Clifford's parable). That she does so with such deftness and skill and in such detail, allows her non-Caribbean and non-Jamaican readers, too, to share these worlds and to perhaps anchor their desire to *affiliate* themselves with Jamaican culture more securely in the realities of that culture. Earlier in this study, I cited a stanza from one of Senior's poems in which she asserts emphatically that ancestry is a matter of *choice*, not of *lineage*:

> My spirit ancestors are those
> I choose to worship and that
> includes an I that existed
> long before me.
>
> (*TT*: 11)

With Clifford's parable in mind, I would suggest that Senior's *Encyclopedia of Jamaican Heritage* provides cultural context and detailed information which might allow the distinction between who is 'in the know' and who is not, to unravel so that the separation of 'insiders' and 'outsiders' becomes both harder to do *and* less desirable or *necessary*.

In addition to the broader conceptual issues raised by the *Encyclopedia*, it is also worth noting the more practical and immediate uses to which the text is already being put. In

131

Jamaica it has been disseminated to schools and libraries: 500 copies were purchased by the Culture, Health, Arts, Sports and Education Fund for distribution across Jamaica. Mr Cosmo Brown, owner of a popular Negril Beach restaurant is reported on the publisher's website to have described the *Encyclopedia* as 'a feast of facts' and donated 50 copies to schools in Hanover and Westmoreland. On the same website, the Jamaica Library Service's Director, Mrs Patricia Roberts is reported as saying, 'The *Encyclopedia* is like a Bible; every school should have one.' In 2004, the *Encyclopedia* was deemed the best reference book published in Jamaica that year. Presumably many Jamaican school children and Jamaican readers will already be familiar with at least some of the cultural practices and historical moments documented in it but, in addition to learning about aspects of Jamaican culture and history not familiar to them, the *Encyclopedia* confirms the idea that Jamaica's cultural heritage is rich, complex and diverse. In relation to at least one diasporic Jamaican community, it may act, as one London-based reviewer argues, as a corrective to the caricatured representation of Jamaicans and Jamaican culture which prevails in the West: 'Guns, drugs, Rastafarianism, reggae music, sunshine and amusing folk customs – for most people that's Jamaica. This impression is reinforced by an ingrained, racist view of Caribbean identity, which has been a reliable background to corporate salesmanship.'[8]

Finally, the *Encyclopedia of Jamaican Heritage* also provides a useful resource when reading Olive Senior's poetry and fiction, offering definitions or expanding the associations of some of the very many cultural references that inform her texts. Senior's fiction and poetry is criss-crossed with detailed and intimate references to as wide a range of cultural practices and historical moments as there are entries in the *Encyclopedia*. The craft and careful attention to the 'small things' in life – as well as the big historical events in which these small stories are embedded – is a distinguishing feature of Olive Senior's oeuvre. The patient research required to collate and complete the *Encyclopedia* is echoed in the careful crafting of the poems and short stories and in the painstaking attention to detail evident in all her work. Rachel Manley's concluding remarks in her review of *Over the Roofs of the World* and the *Encyclopedia* emphatically endorses this point: 'To this, the essential naming with our own names, Olive Senior's fiction, non-fiction, and poetry has made an invaluable contribution, and we welcome these most recent additions.'[9]

## WRITING (ABOUT) THE CARIBBEAN

It is clear from the preceding discussion of poetry and short fiction that Senior is concerned with Caribbean/Jamaican history and culture and seriously committed to representing it in her work in all its complexity. As she says in an interview, 'But everything I write is about the Caribbean, I've never written another word about anywhere else.'[10] Many of the poems present observations about contemporary Caribbean/Jamaican life and culture within the broad context of the region's history of violent conquest and colonial exploitation through to the mixed benefits of independence and the present postcolonial moment. The short stories, for the most part, focus on the immediate, lived realities of particular (often, rural) Jamaican subjects living 'ordinary' lives in the late colonial and early independence periods of Jamaica's history. Alison Donnell argues: 'Both in her short fiction and her poetry, Senior elects a tight locational frame in which to recuperate the lives of those who remain excluded, unknown and significantly unknowable by the metropolitan narratives and metanarratives.'[11]

In the stories and poems, particular Caribbean/Jamaican cultural practices or traditions are seldom 'explained'. Occasionally, notes are provided to assist those readers not familiar with the Caribbean while in other instances the gist of the meaning of particular references becomes apparent in the context of the text as a whole. Senior's writing inscribes a reader already intimately acquainted with the Caribbean/Jamaica, or else one willing to immerse her/himself in the textual world to allow that intimate acquaintance to develop cumulatively in the process of reading. The role of the writer implied in this body of writing, then, is that of a committed chronicler of her country and region. Senior states this straightforwardly:

> But also I write because as a human being, as a Jamaican with a strong commitment to my homeland, I want to reaffirm those parts of our heritage that have been misplaced, misappropriated,

subsumed, submerged, never acknowledged fully as the source of our strength; I want people to know that 'literature' can be created out of the fabric of our everyday lives, that our stories are as worth telling as those of Shakespeare – or the creators of *Dallas*.[12]

Here, the cultural specificity of local cultural forms and practices occupies a somewhat embattled position in relation to global cultural forces. Senior suggests that an explicit commitment to a geographically locatable place and to the specific, detailed cultural practices and stories associated with that place, is a necessary strategy to ensure the survival of what is distinctive about Jamaican culture. This does not imply an unreflective promotion of nationalism for Senior's writing is always attentive to the small stories of individual Jamaican subjects whose lives involve struggles of various kinds *against* national *and* global pressures. In doing so, Senior's work continues an emphasis on representing 'the people' or 'the peasantry' which was char-acteristic of the first wave Caribbean writers in their efforts to construct a distinctively Caribbean literature. While it would be accurate to speak of Senior's themes as 'peasant' in that she does often focus on the ordinary, rural Jamaican subject, it is only possible to do so through a *cumulative* reading of the short stories. That is, she does not offer an explicit construction of 'the peasantry' as a collective constituency but leaves the reader to work out the politics informing her representation of *particular, individual* 'peasants'. The fact that most of her stories are narrated from within 'peasant' communities, and that she seldom deploys omniscient narrators consolidates this effect.

Clearly, Senior, like many of her contemporaries, is writing *after* the manifest failure of postcolonial Jamaican governments to deliver social justice. The unity provided by anti-colonial struggle was ruptured by deep divisions and factionalism in Jamaican politics (and elsewhere in the region). Given these circumstances, Senior is understandably cautious of writing on behalf of any *collective* grouping of 'the people' or 'nation'. In response to a question about the complications of living *outside* of the region despite making it the subject of her work, Senior offers this reply, 'the writer's country is writing and that seems to apply to me.'[13] But, the fact remains that her work contains very little reference to anywhere else *but* the Caribbean. She has not, in other words, written directly about her experience of relocating from Jamaica to Canada. Indeed, the blurb on the back of *Gardening in the Tropics* is forced to pounce on a minute reference to 'snow' (as a counterpoint to the speaker's brightly coloured shoes in 'My Father's Blue Plantation', (*GT*: 84–5)) to convince the prospective Canadian buyer that these poems are for *them*! Senior has remained committed to locating her work *within* the Caribbean. This might be read as a refusal to embrace the 'fashionably multicultural' and to write against the grain of the popular, contemporary representation of the Caribbean subject as emblematic of our contemporary mobile, cross-cultural, hybrid moment. Alison Donnell, mindful of the way that Black Atlantic, diasporic and postcolonial discourses privilege the Caribbean as '*cultural* construction' over its '*geographical* location', warns that, 'it would be both misleading and unfortunate if we allowed the discourse of diaspora to move us away from the Caribbean as a real location.'[14] This need not necessarily imply that there is consensus about how the Caribbean as a 'real location' might be mapped or defined. In relation to Senior's writing, I would see the specificity of location within her work as providing 'a brake' on the tendency for the Caribbean to operate as an infinitely elastic metaphor for abstract notions of hybridity. Her stories and poems chart the impact of History on place: in a sense, they anchor history *in* geography. And her stories insist on the impact of history and geography on the *lived* experiences of Jamaican and Caribbean people. The commitment to documenting these harsh post-colonial realities implies a writer intent on 'bearing witness', a role indicated powerfully in the concluding stanza of Derek Walcott's 'Mass Man':

> Upon your penitential morning,
> some skull must rub its memory with ashes,
> some mind must squat down howling in your dust,
> some hand must crawl and recollect your rubbish,
> *someone must write your poems.*[15]

The 'leap of faith' involved in this commitment to writing perhaps requires even more of a 'leap' in the context of Caribbean nations where populations are small, levels of literacy are generally low, and literary culture fairly circumscribed. As Senior puts it in an interview conducted while she was still resident in Jamaica, 'In Jamaica there is generally an absence of outlets for our work [...] So to stay at home and write is a considerable act of faith.'[16] In the Caribbean, it is still the case that writing and a career as a writer or 'thinker' are generally viewed with suspicion or disbelief or an indication that something is wrong: 'In our societies, people who think too much, or study too hard, or read too much, are thought to be courting madness; mental illness is what results from too much inner contemplation.'[17]

A more 'practical' but equally dismissive attitude, suggests that unless it is *economically* viable writing is a pointless process. For the woman writer, there is the added suspicion that writing displaces her 'proper' vocation as mother and wife. In an interview Senior describes the responses she met when she told friends about the publication of her first book (on the 1972 general election in Jamaica): 'She said, "A book?" and roared with laughter. After that book was published to good critical and public reception, an old school mate saw me and asked what I was doing with myself. I said, "Writing." She dismissed that instantly. "Writing?" she said as if I had said whoring. "So when are you going to settle down and have children?"'[18] Despite the deep suspicions attendant on being a writer, Senior has continued to make her living from writing and activities related to writing – creative writing workshops, lectures reading tours and so on – in the Caribbean, as well as in Europe and North America.

Olive Senior's extensive oeuvre provides the region with careful and patiently inscribed representations of Jamaican people and culture. Her work also signals the possibilities for a more understated register and a quieter 'voice' than is usually associated with the region's writing. While there is currently a great deal of critical investment in discourses of 'slackness' and 'rude bwai talk' as models of Caribbean resistance, Olive Senior's work inscribes 'resistance' with craft and careful cunning to produce subtle and often surprisingly powerful effects. Taken as a whole, her writing across the genres discussed in this study, offers sustained insights into what it means to be a Caribbean subject living in a postcolonial world. Her body of work and her own commentary on that work also provides suggestive models of the committed, 'organic' intellectual and cultural activist.

In her introduction to *Encyclopedia of Jamaican Heritage*, Senior suggests that Jamaicans 'are not newly minted and fashionably "multicultural"', and she offers an account of a creolizing process that is altogether slower and less spectacular than we have come to associate with discourses of hybridity:

> Though we might be able to trace this or that element of our heritage to Africa, or the British Isles, the transforming genius of place is such that we have over centuries managed to infuse whatever we import with our own desires, adapt it to our needs, graft it on to what is indigenous, so that ultimately it becomes a reflection of who we are, our 'version', named with our own names. (*EJH*: ix)

Olive Senior's writing provides detailed, patient and loving excavation of these complicated and contradictory cultural forms so that our version(s) of Jamaican, Caribbean and, by extension, postcolonial realities can be rendered in more nuanced ways – and 'named with our own names'.

137

# Notes

## CHAPTER 1. LOCATING OLIVE SENIOR'S WORK

1. Dolace McClean and Jacqueline Bishop, 'Of Hearts Revealed: An Interview with Olive Senior', *Callaloo* 2.2 (Summer/Fall, 2003), 3–13, p.6.

2. George Lamming, 'Concepts of the Caribbean', in Frank Birbalsingh (ed.), *Frontiers of Caribbean Literature in English* (London and Basingstoke: Macmillan, 1996), 2.

3. Jean Besson, 'Reputation and Respectability Reconsidered: A New Perspective on Afro-Caribbean Women', in Janet H. Momsen (ed.): *Women and Change in the Caribbean* (Kingston: Ian Randle, 1993), 30. Richard Burton, writing over two decades after Wilson in 1997, acknowledges the male emphasis of his own study, *Afro-Creole: Power, Opposition and Play in the Caribbean*, indicating perhaps a sense of the difficulty of short-circuiting a predominantly male-oriented archive.

4. Two among many other influential texts that inaugurated this shift in historiography are Hilary Beckles, *Natural Rebels: A Social History of Enslaved Black Women* (1989) and Barbara Bush, *Slave Women in Caribbean Society: 1650–1838* (1990).

5. Franz Fanon, *The Wretched of the Earth* (Harmondsworth: Penguin, 1967), 167.

6. George Lamming, *The Pleasures of Exile* (London and New York: Alison and Busby, 1984), 29.

7. George Lamming, 'The Peasant Roots of the West Indian Novel', in Edward Baugh (ed.), *Critics on Caribbean Literature* (London: Allen & Unwin, 1978), 25.

8. V. S. Naipaul, *The Middle Passage: The Caribbean Revisited* (London: Penguin, 1969), 73.

9. Derek Walcott, *What the Twilight Says: Essays* (London: Faber, 1998), 37.

10. Gordon Rohlehr, 'West Indian Poetry: Some Problems of Assessment', *Bim*, 54 & 55 (1971), 83.

11. Laurence Breiner, 'How to Behave on Paper: The *Savacou* Debate', *Journal of West Indian Literature* 6.1 (1993), 1–10, p.3.
12. Paula Burnett, *The Penguin Book of Caribbean Verse in English* (London: Penguin, 1986), 70.
13. Derek Walcott, *Collected Poems 1948–1984* ([1986] New York: The Noon Day Press, 1990), 88.
14. Naipaul, *Middle Passage*, 29.
15. Edward Kamau Brathwaite, *The Arrivants: A New World Trilogy* ([1967] Oxford: Oxford University Press, 1981), 48.
16. See Evelyn O'Callaghan's *Women Writing the West Indies 1804–1939: 'A Hot Place Belonging to Us'* (London: Routledge, 2004) for discussion of a range of early texts by women.
17. J. Edward Chamberlin, *Come Back To Me My Language: Poetry and the West Indies* (Toronto: McClelland, 1993), 95.
18. Burnett, *Penguin Book*, p. xxxix.
19. Olive Senior, in Marlies Glaser and Marion Pausch (eds.), *Caribbean Writers: Between Orality and Writing* (Amsterdam–Atlanta: Rodopi, 1994), 82.
20. Ifeoma Kiddoe Nwankwo, 'Introduction', *Journal of West Indian Literature* 6.20 (2009), pp.viii–xxv, p. viii.
21. Grace Nichols, *i is a long memoried woman* (London: Karnak House, 1983), 50.
22. See e.g. Henry Louis Gates Jr., *The Signifying Monkey: A Theory of African-American Literary Criticism* (Oxford: OUP, 1988).
23. Louise Bennett, *Selected Poems*, ed. Mervyn Morris (Kingston: Sangsters, 1982), 21–2.
24. Pamela Mordecai and Mervyn Morris (eds.), *Jamaica Woman: An Anthology of Poems* ([1980] London, Kingston, Port of Spain: Heinemann, 1985), p. xi.
25. 'Dougla' in Caribbean Creole refers, literally, to the offspring of African and Indian parentage.
26. See e.g. Brinda Mehta, *Diasporic (Dis)Locations: Indo-Caribbean Women Writers Negotiate the Kala Pani* (Kingston: University of West Indies Press, 2004) and Shalini Puri, *The Caribbean Postcolonial: Social Equality, Post-Nationalism, and Cultural Hybridity* (New York and Basingtoke: Palgrave and Macmillan, 2004).
27. See Ch. 4 in Alison Donnell, *Twentieth-Century Caribbean Literature: Critical Moments in Anglophone Literary History* (London: Routledge, 2006) for a detailed discussion of this.
28. Honor Ford-Smith (ed.), *Lionheart Gal: Life Stories of Jamaican Women* ([1986] Kingston: University of West Indies Press, 2005), 289.
29. Ibid. 289.
30. See Denise deCaires Narain, Alison Donnell and Evelyn O'Callaghan, 'Sex, Text and the Caribbean Body: Beyond the Spectacle of

Heteronormativity' in Hyacinth Simpson (ed.), *Caribbean Migrations: Essays on Diaspora and Transnationalism* (Newcastle: Cambridge Scholars Publishing), forthcoming.

31. James Clifford, *The Predicament of Culture: Twentieth-Century Ethnography, Literature and Art* (Cambridge, Mass: Harvard University Press, 1988), 173.

32. Laura Tanner, 'One-on-one with Olive Senior' in *Jamaica Gleaner*,17 October 2004. *http://www.jamaica-gleaner.com/gleaner/20041017/arts/arts3.html* n. p.

33. Charles H. Rowell, 'An Interview with Olive Senior', *Callaloo* 11.3 (Summer 1988), 480–90, p.482.

34. Ibid. 487.

35. Jan Shinebourne, 'Fragments of People, Fragments of Culture', *Everywoman* (June 1991), 20–2, p.22.

## CHAPTER 2. THE STORY AS GOSSIP: CREOLIZING THE TEXT

1. Olive Senior, 'The Poem as Gardening, The Story as Su-Su: Finding a Literary Voice' in *Journal of West Indian Literature* 14 1–2 (2005), 37.

2. Ibid. 46–7.

3. Stewart Brown, in his Introduction, Stewart Brown and John Wickham (eds.), *The Oxford Book of Caribbean Short Stories* (Oxford: OUP, 1999), p. xxviii, describes this story as 'one of the finest comic moments in the whole literature'.

4. Hyacinth Simpson, 'Voicing the text: the Making of an Oral Poetics in Olive Senior's Short Stories', *Callaloo* 27.3 (2004), 836.

5. Oliver Senior interview with Marlies Glaser in Marlies Glaser and Maron Pusch (eds.), *Caribbean Writers: Between Orality and Writing* (Amsterdam-Atlanta: Rodopi, 1994), 82.

6. Olive Senior's *Working Miracles* also attests to this, see p.39, for example.

7. Helen Gilbert, '"Let them know you have broughtuptcy": Childhood and Child-Subjects in Olive Senior's Short Stories', *Kunapipi* xxvi.i (2004), 24–38, p.24.

8. George Lamming's *In the Castle of My Skin* might be read as a 'classic' example of a Caribbean *bildungsroman*.

9. Simpson, 'Voicing the text', 835.

10. Gilbert, 'Let them know', 27.

11. Here, the balmyard is presented as an indigenous cultural practice which has none of the more dangerous association of 'obeah' practices.

## CHAPTER 3. NEGOTIATING 'DIFFERENCE': FEMININITY, MASCULINITY, ETHNICITY

1. Brand, Dionne, *Bread Out of Stone: Sex, Recognition, Race, Dreaming, Politics* (Toronto: Coach House, 1994), 27.
2. Texts by Patricia Powell, Laurence Scott, Shani Mootoo, Thomas Glave and many others have contributed to this 'queering' of Caribbean literature.
3. Jean Rhys, *Wide Sargasso Sea* (London: Penguin, 1966), 38.
4. Adrienne Rich, 'Compulsory Heterosexuality and Lesbian Existence' in *Blood, Bread, and Poetry: Selected Prose 1979–1985* (Norton Paperback: New York, 1994).
5. Alison Donnell, 'Hybrid Bodies: Theorizing the Body That will Not Fit in Olive Senior's Short Stories', *Journal of the Short Story in English* 26 (Spring 1996), 38–48, p.41.
6. Edward Kamau Brathwaite, *The Development of Creole Society 1770–1820* (Oxford: Clarendon Press, 1971), 305.
7. Chin, Timothy, '"Bullers" and "Battymen": Contesting Homophobia in Black Popular Contemporary Caribbean Literature', *Callaloo* 20.1 (1997), 127–41, p. 285.
8. Space does not permit me to pursue this here but I do so in detail in a current work-in-progress, 'Queorying Queer Caribbean Paradigms: a Tentative Return to Creolization'.
9. This is a scenario intriguingly reminiscent of the opening of Thomas Hardy's novel, *The Mayor of Casterbridge*.
10. Ameena Gafoor, 'The Image of the Indo-Caribbean Woman in Olive Senior's "The [sic] Arrival of the Snake Woman"', *Callaloo* 16.1 (Winter 1993), 34–43, p.35.
11. The Tulsi women are viewed collectively by Mohun Biswas as a powerful dominating force controlling all activity in Hanuman House under the scrutiny of the matriarch, Mrs Tulsi. V. S. Naipaul, *A House For Mr Biswas* (London: Penguin, 1961).
12. Gafoor, 'The Image of the Indo-Caribbean Woman', 39.
13. Ibid. 39.
14. Ibid. 36.
15. Ibid. 39.
16. R. Kanhai, *Matikor: The Politics of Identity for Indo-Caribbean Women* (St Augustine, Trinidad: University of West Indies School of Continuing Studies, 1999), p. xii.
17. Brinda Mehta, *Diasporic (Dis)Locations: Indi-Caribbean Women Writers Negotiate the Kala Pani* (Kingston: University of West Indies Press, 2004), 2.
18. One might read the way Mr da Silva's hands, 'ugly and thickly

covered with matted hair like some wild beast' (*ASW*: 121) function in 'Lily, Lily', as the most intense symbol of his inappropriate interest in his adopted child. In the absence of other representations of Portuguese subjects, his 'swarthy' hands come to symbolize (rather uncomfortably) *both* his perverse sexuality *and* his ethnic difference.

19. Nigel Bolland, 'Creolization and Creole Societies' in *Intellectuals in the Twentieth-Century Caribbean*, ed. Alistair Hennessy (London and Basingstoke: Macmillan Caribbean, 1992), 53.

## CHAPTER 4. NATURE STUDIES: OLIVE SENIOR'S 'DOWN-TO-EARTH' ECO-POETICS

1. Edouard Glissant, *Caribbean Discourse: Selected Essays*. Translated by J. Michael Dash (Charlottesville: University of Virginia Press, 1989), 11.
2. Elizabeth M. DeLoughrey, Renée K. Gosson and George B. Handley (eds.), *Caribbean Literature and the Environment: Between Nature and Culture* ([written 1973] Charlottesville and London: University of Virginia Press, 2005), 1.
3. Lloyd Brown, *West Indian Poetry* (London: Heinemann, 1984), 23.
4. Derek Walcott, 'Isla Incognita', in Elizabeth M. DeLoughrey, Renée K. Gosson and George B. Handley (eds.), *Caribbean Literature and the Environment: Between Nature and Culture* (Charlottesville and London: University of Virginia Press), 55, my emphasis.
5. Edward Kamau Brathwaite, *Roots* (Ann Arbor: University of Michigan Press, 1993), 265.
6. V. S. Naipaul, *The Middle Passage: The Caribbean Revisited* (London: Penguin, 1969), 67.
7. Helen Tiffin, '"Man Fitting the Landscape"': Nature, Culture and Colonialism', in DeLoughrey et al., *Caribbean Literature and the Environment*, 200.
8. There is concern currently that Cockpit Country itself is under threat by plans to mine for bauxite there. See *http://www.jeanjamaica.org/documents/Save%20Cockpit%20Country%20Fact%20-Sheet%202007.pdf* for a factsheet on the 'Save Cockpit Country' appeal organized by the NGO, Jamaica Environmental Advocacy Network.
9. Mimi Sheller, *Consuming the Caribbean: From Arawaks to Zombies* (London: Routledge, 2003), 13. See also, Richard Drayton's *Nature's Government: Science, Imperial Britain, and the 'Improvement' of the World* for a broader and more complex study of global networks of

scientific research and knowledge production.

10. Jamaica Kincaid, *A Small Place* (London: Virago, 1988), 18–19.

11. It strikes me that when an Amerindian presence is invoked in Caribbean poetry, it tends to be in heroic, memorializing or nostalgic modes, a tendency Senior avoids.

12. *http://www.jamaicans.com/culture/folk/isaw.shtml*; accessed 13.9.2010.

13. In Guyana's Botanical gardens, for example, the statue of Queen Victoria which had been a feature of the gardens during the colonial era, was moved from its central position and left abandoned on its back for many months, spawning numerous suggestive jokes and innuendoes.

14. Jamaica Kincaid, *My Garden (Book)* (London: Vintage, 2000), 90.

15. Glissant, *Caribbean Discourse*, 11.

16. DeLoughrey et al, *Caribbean Literature and the Environment*, 2–3.

17. Senior acknowledges (p.136) Richard Price's *Maroon Societies: Rebel Slave Communities in the Americas* (New York: Anchor), 1973.

18. Derek Walcott, *What the Twilight Says: Essays* (London: Faber, 1998), 37.

19. Hena Maes-Jelinek, 'From Living Nature to Borderless Culture In Wilson Harris's Work', in DeLoughrey et al., *Caribbean Literature and the Environment*, 247.

20. Edouard Glissant, *Poetics of Relation*. Trans., Betsy Wing ([1990] Ann Arbor: University of Michigan Press, 2005), 147, my emphasis.

21. Jordon Stouck, 'Gardening in the Diaspora', in *Mosaic* 38.4 (2005), 103–23, p.120.

22. Derek Walcott, *Collected Poems 1948–1984* ([1986] New York: The Noon Day Press, 1990), 364.

23. Brathwaite, *The Arrivants*, p.34; his emphasis throughout the trilogy is on the travails of the black *male* subject.

24. Laura Tanner, 'One-on-one with Olive Senior', *Jamaica Gleaner*, 17 October 2004, n.p.

25. In 'Swimming in the Ba'ma Grass' (*DH*: 83–91) the man who follows his beloved to a landlocked village, remembers the beauty of the sea with intense longing.

26. The poem's title is arranged so that 'CANOE' is underlined and OCEAN lies beneath it.

27. Walt Whitman, *Leaves of Grass* ([c 1900] Philadelphia: David McKay); Bartleby.com, 1999. www.bartleby.com/142/. [Accessed 03.08.10] n.p.

28. The intertextual parallel here is with the following lines from Act 1 Scene 1:
Prospero:           Thou most lying slave,
Whom stripes may move, not kindness! I have us'd thee
Filth as thou art, with human care; and lodg'd thee

In mine own cell, till thou didst seek to violate
The honour of my child [Miranda]
Caliban: O ho, O ho! Would't had been done!
Thou didst prevent me; I had peopled else
This isle with Calibans.

29. Rod Edmond and Vanessa Smith, *Islands in History and Representation* (London: Routledge, 2003), 1.
30. Walcott, *Collected Poems*, 294.
31. Ibid. 72; see also Walcott's play, *Pantomime* for sharply satirical reprise of the Crusoe-castaway narrative.
32. Homi Bhabha, *The Location of Culture* (London: Routledge, 1994), 67.
33. Kincaid, *A Small Place*, 31–2.
34. Dolace McClean and Jacqueline Bishop, 'Of Hearts Revealed: An Interview with Olive Senior', *Callaloo* 2.2 (Summer/Fall 2003), 7.

## CHAPTER 5. SPINNING A YARN: LABOURING LIVES, MIGRATION STORIES AND THE WRITER'S CRAFT

1. Anne Collett, 'Blue Be-Longing: A Discussion of Olive Senior's Latest Collection of Poetry, *Over the Roofs of the World*', *Ariel* 37.2–3 (2006), 221–35, p.226.
2. Both 're-memory' and 'the unspeakable' nature of slavery are terms associated with several of Toni Morrison's works.
3. Honor Ford-Smith (ed.), *Lionheart Gal: Life Stories of Jamaican Women* ([1986] Kingston: University of West Indies Press, 2005), 289.
4. Amryl Johnson, *Long Road To Nowhere* (London: Virago, 1985), 39.
5. Higglers are women who are involved in small-scale retail trade: produce from small farms but increasingly also a variety of portable consumer goods purchased in Miami for resale in the islands. They have considerable economic power and are associated with formidable vocal power.
6. In Jamaica, 'solomon a Grundy' also refers to a popular, peppery fishpaste.
7. See Paule Marshall's *Praisesong for the Widow* for a literary inscription of this story.
8. Labour was recruited from the West Indies (and other colonies) following WW2 to work in Britain's transport and health industries.
9. Alison Donnell, *Twentieth-Century Caribbean Literature: Critical Moments in Anglophone Literary History* (Routledge: London, 2006), 104.
10. Salman Rushdie, *The Satanic Verses* (London and New York: Viking, 1988), 8.
11. 'Ol' Higue' in Caribbean folklore refers to a witch who sheds her

skin at night and flies in the shape of a bat in search of human blood. It is also used to describe someone who 'nags'.

12. In 1794 eleven Ursuline nuns from Valenciennes were accused of treachery and sent to the guillotine but the poem does not appear to refer directly to these events.

13. Edward Kamau Brathwaite, *The Development of Creole Society 1770–1820* (Oxford: Clarendon Press, 1971), 38. For a succinct overview of these debates by Peter Hulme, followed by E. K. Brathwaite's response, and a further commentary by Elaine Savory Fido, Evelyn O'Callaghan and Denise deCaires Narain, see *Wasafiri* 20 (Autumn 1994), 5–11; *Wasafiri* 21 (Spring 1995), 69–78; *Wasafiri* 28 (Autumn 1998), 33–8.

14. This resonates with the lines in 'Embroidery' in which the speaker recognizes the way that her aunts, under 'cover' of their sedate embroidery, 'bad talk' Aunt Millie. The speaker sells the pearls her Aunt Millie leaves her and 'becomes a blue foot traveller./ Kept no diary. Sewed up my mouth. Shunned embroidery.' (*ORW*: 79)

## CHAPTER 6. THE WRITER AS CULTURAL ARCHIVIST: OLIVE SENIOR'S NON-FICTION WORKS

1. Charles H. Rowell, 'An Interview with Olive Senior', *Callaloo* 11.3 (Summer 1988), 483.

2. Anna Rutherford, 'Interview with Olive Senior' in *Kunapapi* viii (1986), 11–20, p.15.

3. 'Bluefoot traveller' is a phrase used to describe Jamaicans who leave their island and then return.

4. Dolace McClean and Jacqueline Bishop, 'Of Hearts Revealed: An Interview with Olive Senior', *Callaloo* 2.2 (Summer/Fall 2003), 8.

5. Jan Shinebourne, 'Fragments of People, Fragments of Culture', *Everywoman* (June 1991), 22.

6. Clifford, James, 'On Ethnographic Allegory' in James Clifford and George E. Marcus (eds.), *Writing Culture: The Poetics and Politics of Ethnography* (Berkeley: University of California Press, 1986), 116.

7. Ibid.

8. Phillips, Mike, Review of *Encyclopedia of Jamaican Heritage*, *Guardian*, 26 February 2005: http://books.guardian.co.uk/review/story/0,,1424565,00.html

9. Rachel Manley, 'Secrets and Names', *Caribbean Review of Books* (August 2005), 22–4, p.24.

10. McClean and Bishop, 'Of Hearts Revealed', 6.

11. Alison Donnell, *Twentieth-Century Caribbean Literature: Critical Mo-*

*ments in Anglophone Literary History* (London: Routledge, 2006), 95.

12. Rowell, 'An Interview with Olive Senior', 484.
13. McClean and Bishop, 'Of Hearts Revealed', 6.
14. Donnell, *Twentieth-Century Caribbean Literature*, 94.
15. DerekWalcott, *Collected Poems 1948–1984* ([1986] New York: The Noon Day Press, 1990), 99.
16. Rowell, 'An Interview with Olive Senior', 486.
17. Jan Shinebourne, 'Fragments of People, Fragments of Culture', *Everywoman* (June 1991), 21.
18. Rowell, 'An Interview with Olive Senior', 481.

# Select Bibliography

## WORKS BY OLIVE SENIOR

### Poetry

*Talking of Trees* (Kingston: Calabash, 1985).
*Gardening in the Tropics* (Toronto: McClelland & Stewart, 1994).
*Over the Roofs of the World* (Toronto: Insomniac Press, 2005).
*Shell* (Toronto: Insomniac Press, 2007).

### Short Stories

*Summer Lightning and Other Stories* (London: Longman, 1986).
*Arrival of the Snake-Woman and Other Stories* (London, Longman, 1989).
*Discerner of Hearts and Other Stories* (Toronto: McClelland & Stewart, 1995).

### Non-Fiction Works

*A–Z of Jamaican Heritage* (Kingston: Heinemann and the Gleaner Company Ltd, 1984).
*Working Miracles: Women's Lives in the English-Speaking Caribbean* (London: James Curry; Bloomington: Indiana University Press, 1991).
*Encyclopedia of Jamaican Heritage* (Kingston: Twin Guinep Publishers, 2004).
'The Poem as Gardening, The Story as Su-Su: Finding a Literary Voice' in *Journal of West Indian Literature* 14.1–2 (2005).

## INTERVIEWS WITH OLIVE SENIOR

McClean, Dolace and Jacqueline Bishop, 'Of Hearts Revealed: An Interview with Olive Senior', *Callaloo* 2.2 (Summer/Fall 2003), 3–13.

Rowell, Charles H., 'An Interview with Olive Senior', *Callaloo* 11.3 (Summer 1988), 480–90.

Rutherford, Anna, 'Olive Senior: Interview', *Kunapipi* 8.2 (1986), 11–20.

Shinebourne, Jan, 'Fragments of People, Fragments of Culture', *Everywoman* (June 1991), 20–2.

Simpson, Hyacinth, 'The In-Between Worlds of Olive Senior: An Interview', *Wasafiri* 53 (Spring 2008), 10–15.

Tanner, Laura 'One-on-one with Olive Senior', *Jamaica Gleaner*, 17 October 2004, *http://www.jamaica-gleaner.com/gleaner/20041017/arts/arts3.html*

## GENERAL BIBLIOGRAPHY

Bennett, Louise, *Selected Poems* ed. Mervyn Morris (Kingston: Sangsters, 1982).

Besson, Jean, 'Reputation and Respectability Reconsidered: A New Perspective on Afro-Caribbean Women' in Janet H. Momsen (ed.), *Women and Change in the Caribbean* (Kingston: Ian Randle, 1993).

Bhabha, Homi, *The Location of Culture* (London: Routledge, 1994).

Brand, Dionne, *Bread Out of Stone: Sex, Recognition, Race, Dreaming, Politics*, (Toronto: Coach House, 1994).

Bolland, Nigel, Creolization and Creole Societies in *Intellectuals in the Twentieth-Century Caribbean*, ed. Alistair Hennessy (London and Basingstoke: Macmillan Caribbean, 1992).

Brathwaite, Edward Kamau, *Roots* (Ann Arbor: University of Michigan Press, 1993).

———, *The Arrivants: A New World Trilogy* ([1967] Oxford: Oxford University Press, 1981).

———, *The Development of Creole Society 1770–1820* (Oxford: Clarendon Press, 1971).

Breiner, Laurence, 'How to Behave on Paper': The *Savacou* Debate: *Journal of West Indian Literature* 6.1 (1993), 1–10.

Brown, Lloyd, *West Indian Poetry* (London: Heinemann, 1984).

Burman, Jenny, 'Remittance; Or, Diasporic Economies of Yearning', *Small Axe* 6.2 (2002), 49–71.

Burnett, Paula, *The Penguin Book of Caribbean Verse in English* (London: Penguin, 1986).

Burton, Richard, *Afro-Creole: Power, Opposition and Play in the Caribbean* (Ithaca and London: Cornell University Press, 1997).

Chamberlin, J. Edward, *Come Back To Me My Language: Poetry and the West Indies* (Toronto: McClelland, 1993).

Chin, Timothy, ' "Bullers" and "Battymen": Contesting Homophobia in Black Popular Contemporary Caribbean literature', *Callaloo* 20.1

(1997), 127–41.

Clifford, James, 'On Ethnographic Allegory' in James Clifford and George E. Marcus (eds.), *Writing Culture: The Poetics and Politics of Ethnography* (Berkeley: University of California Press, 1986).

———, The Predicament of Culture: Twentieth-Century Ethnography, Literature and Art (Cambridge, Mass: Harvard University Press, 1988).

Collett, Anne, 'Gardening in the Tropics: A Horticultural Guide to Caribbean Politics', *SPAN* 46 (April 1998).

———, '"And Woman's Tongue Clatters out of Turn": Olive Senior's Praise Song for Woman-weed', *Kunapipi* 20.2 (1999).

———,'Blue Be-Longing: A Discussion of Olive Senior's Latest Collection of Poetry, *Over the Roofs of the World'*, *Ariel* 37.2–3 (2006), 221–35.

Conde, Mary 'Unlikely Stories: Children's Invented Worlds in Caribbean Women's Fiction', *Commonwealth Essays and Studies* 1 (Autumn 1992), 69–75.

Cooper, Carolyn, *Noises in the Blood: Orality, Gender and the 'Vulgar' Body of Jamaican Popular Culture* (London: Macmillan, 1993).

DeLoughrey, Elizabeth, Renée K. Gosson and George B. Handley (eds.), *Caribbean Literature and the Environment: Between Nature and Culture* ([written 1973] Charlottesville and London: University of Virginia Press, 2005).

Donnell, Alison, 'Hybrid Bodies: Theorizing the Body That will Not Fit in Olive Senior's Short Stories', *Journal of the Short Story in English* 26 (Spring 1996), 38–48.

———, 'Here and There in the Work of Olive Senior: Relocating Diaspora Discourse in Relation to Caribbean Women's Writing', *Centre of Remembrance: Memory and Caribbean Women's Literature*, ed. Joan Anim-Ado (London: Mango Publishing, 2002).

———, Twentieth-Century Caribbean Literature: Critical Moments in Anglophone Literary History (London: Routledge, 2006).

Edmond, Rod and Vanessa Smith, *Islands in History and Representation* (London: Routledge, 2003).

Fanon, Franz, *The Wretched of the Earth* (Harmondsworth: Penguin, 1967).

Ford-Smith, Honor (ed.), *Lionheart Gal: Life Stories of Jamaican Women* ([1986] Kingston: University of West Indies Press, 2005).

Gafoor Ameena 'The Image of the Indo-Caribbean Woman in Olive Senior's "The [sic] Arrival of the Snake Woman"', *Callaloo* 16.1 (Winter 1993), 34–43.

Gates, Henry Louis Jr., *The Signifying Monkey: A Theory of African-American Literary Criticism* (Oxford: Oxford University Press, 1988).

Gilbert, Helen, '"Let them know you have broughtuptcy": Childhood and Child-Subjects in Olive Senior's Short Stories', *Kunapipi* 26.1 (2004), 24–38.

Glaser, Marlies and Marion Pausch (eds.), *Caribbean Writers: Between Orality and Writing* (Amsterdam–Atlanta: Rodopi, 1994).

Glissant, Edouard, *Caribbean Discourse: Selected Essays*. Translated by J. Michael Dash (Charlottesville: University of Virginia Press, 1989).

————, *Poetics of Relation*. Translated by Betsy Wing ([1990] Ann Arbor: University of Michigan Press, 2005).

Grove, Richard, *Green Imperialism: Colonial Expansion, Tropical Island Edens and the Origins of Environmentalism* (Cambridge and New York: Cambridge University Press, 1995).

Johnson, Amryl, *Long Road to Nowhere* (London: Virago, 1985).

Kanhai, Rosanne, *Matikor: The Politics of Identity for Indo-Caribbean Women* (St Augustine, Trinidad: University of West Indies School of Continuing Studies, 1999).

Kincaid, Jamaica, *A Small Place* (London: Virago, 1988).

————, *My Garden (Book)* (London: Vintage, 2000).

Lamming, George, 'The Peasant Roots of the West Indian Novel' in Edward Baugh, *Critics on Caribbean Literature* (London: Allen & Unwin, 1978).

————, *The Pleasures of Exile* ([1960] London and New York: Alison and Busby, 1984).

————, 'Concepts of the Caribbean' in Frank Birbalsingh (ed.), *Frontiers of Caribbean Literature in English* (London and Basingstoke: Macmillan, 1996).

Manley, Rachel, 'Secrets and Names', *Caribbean Review of Books* (August 2005), 22–4.

McClean, Dolace and Bishop Brinda Mehta, *Diasporic (Dis)Locations: Indi-Caribbean Women Writers Negotiate the Kala Pani* (Kingston: University of West Indies Press, 2004).

Mordecai, Pamela and Mervyn Morris (eds.), *Jamaica Woman: An Anthology of Poems* ([1980] London, Kingston, Port of Spain: Heinemann, 1985).

Naipaul, V. S., *The Middle Passage: The Caribbean Revisited* (London: Penguin, 1969).

Nichols, Grace, *i is a long memoried woman* (London: Karnak House, 1983).

Nwankwo, Ifeoma Kiddoe, Introduction, *Journal of West Indian Literature* 6.20 (2009), pp. viii–xxv.

O'Callaghan, Evelyn, *Women Writing the West Indies: 'A Hot Place Belonging to Us'* (London: Routledge, 2004).

Phillips, Gyllian, 'Personal and Textual Geographies in Olive Senior's Literary Relationship with Jean Rhys', *Journal of Caribbean Literatures* 3.3 (2003).

Phillips, Mike, review of *Encyclopedia of Jamaican Heritage*, *Guardian*, 26 February 2005. *http://books.guardian.co.uk/review/story/ 0,,1424565,00.html*

Pollard, Velma, 'To Us All Flowers Are Roses: Writing Ourselves Into the Literature of the Caribbean', *Centre of Remembrance: Memory and Caribbean Women's Literature*, ed. Joan Anim-Ado (London: Mango Publishing, 2002).

Prest, John, *The Garden of Eden: The Botanic Garden and the Recreation of Paradise* (New Haven: Yale University Press, 1981).

Puri, Shalini, *The Caribbean Postcolonial: Social Equality, Post-Nationalism, and Cultural Hybridity* (New York and Basingstoke: Palgrave and Macmillan, 2004).

Rhys, Jean, *Wide Sargasso Sea* ([1966] London: Penguin, 1983).

Rohlehr, Gordon, 'West Indian Poetry: Some Problems of Assessment', *Bim* 54 & 55 (1971).

Rushdie, Salman, *The Satanic Verses* (London and New York: Viking, 1988).

Sheller, Mimi, *Consuming the Caribbean: From Arawaks to Zombies* (London: Routledge, 2003).

Simpson, Hyacinth, '"Voicing the Text": The Making of an Oral Poetics in Olive Senior's Short Stories', *Callaloo* 27.3 (2004), 829–43.

Stouck, Jordan, 'Gardening in the Diaspora' in *Mosaic* 38.4 (2005), 103–23.

Tiffin, Helen, 'Flowers of Evil, Flowers of Empire: Roses and Daffodils in the Works of Jamaica Kincaid, Olive Senior and Lorna Goodison', *SPAN* 46 (April 1998).

———, '"Man Fitting the Landscape": Nature, Culture and Colonialism' in *Caribbean Literature and the Environment*, ed. DeLoughrey et al.

Walcott, Derek, *What the Twilight Says: Essays* (London: Faber, 1998).

———, *Collected Poems 1948–1984* ([1986] New York: The Noon Day Press, 1990).

———, 'Isla Incognita' in *Caribbean Literature and the Environment*, ed. DeLoughrey et al.

Whitman, Walt. *Leaves of Grass* (Philadelphia: David McKay c 1900; Bartleby.com, 1999. *www.bartleby.com/142/*. [Accessed 03.08.10].

Wilson, Peter, *Crab Antics: The Social Anthropology of English-Speaking Negro Societies in the Caribbean* (New Haven: Yale University Press, 1973).

# Index

152

Lightning Source UK Ltd.
Milton Keynes UK
UKOW040030070812

197143UK00005B/24/P